A House of Cards

AMERICAN CULTURE

Cutting across traditional boundaries between the human and social sciences, volumes in the American Culture series study the multiplicity of cultural practices from theoretical, historical, and ethnographic perspectives by examining culture's production, circulation, and consumption.

Edited by Stanley Aronowitz, Nancy Fraser, and George Lipsitz

A HOUSE of Cards

BASEBALL CARD COLLECTING AND POPULAR CULTURE

JOHN BLOOM

American Culture, Volume 12

University of Minnesota Press
Minneapolis
London

Published by the University of Minnesota Press
111 Third Avenue South, Suite 290, Minneapolis, MN 55401-2520
Printed in the United States of America on acid-free paper

Library of Congress Cataloging-in-Publication Data

Bloom, John, 1962–
    A house of cards : baseball card collecting and popular culture / John Bloom.
        p.   cm. — (American culture ; v. 12)
    Includes bibliographical references and index.
    ISBN 0-8166-2870-X (hc : alk. paper)
    ISBN 0-8166-2871-8 (pb : alk. paper)
    1. Baseball cards—Collectors and collecting—Social aspects—United States.   2. Popular culture—United States—History.
    3. Men—United States—Psychology.   I. Title.   II. Series: American culture (Minneapolis, Minn.) ; 12.
    GV875.3.B56   1997
    796.357'0973'075—dc20   96-32883

The University of Minnesota is an
equal-opportunity educator and employer.

Only four sparks [remain] in my memory—four images that root me to this epoch: 1) The sound of Don Pardo's booming voice. 2) The sight of Richard Castellano's sister naked. 3) The fear that Albert Dorish might beat me up. 4) My three shopping bags full of baseball cards. (Boyd and Harris 1973, 20) (Authors Brendan Boyd and Fred Harris on the significance of baseball cards to their memories of growing up during the 1950s)

"Consciously, it may just be a love of the sport. . . . Unconsciously, I'm sure for me, it's vicarious. I was never good enough to play. . . . It's also an unconscious search for order in life. You're always aiming to complete a set, and that's a sense of security." (Woodhull 1974) (An adult male baseball card collector interviewed by the Detroit Free Press *at a Detroit baseball card show in 1974)*

"It sounds to me like they're jealous. . . . sure we've ruined their hobby, but isn't that what America is all about?" (I Will Swap 1990) (Baseball card speculator Alan "Mr. Mint" Rosen to the Wall Street Journal *in 1990 on how he and other baseball card profiteers have affected the hobby)*

Contents

Acknowledgments

Had it not been for the constant support and guidance of many people, I am sure that I would never have been able to complete this project, and I certainly would not have comprehended, as much as I have, the richness and complexities of the subculture I studied. I am especially thankful to the baseball card collectors who shared their time and thoughts with me between 1988 and 1991. They managed to meet me at their homes or at restaurants in spite of foul weather or other inconveniences and were always hospitable and open to my questions. Also, numerous baseball card shop owners and show promoters allowed me to distribute questionnaires and to interview collectors at their venues.

I have learned as much from the work and commentary of my peers in this project as I have from anything else. Various friends provided commentary, participated in writing groups, or read early drafts of this book, including Joy Barbre, Catherine Besteman, Ken Dauber, Suzanne Dietzel, Michiko Hase, Jane Healey, Mark Hulsether, Scott Kassner, Tessie Liu, Susan Niles, April Schultz, and Tony Smith. Wendy Kozol's comments, insights, and interest in my work have been especially helpful. Gary Alan Fine, Elaine Tyler May, Lary May, and Riv-Ellen Prell all were valuable mentors for me as well. I am indebted to the School of American Research in Santa Fe, New Mexico, for providing me with a generous predoctoral resident scholar fellowship, funded by the Weatherhead Foundation, which allowed me to complete my dissertation in 1991. I also wish to express my appreciation to Krause Publications of Iola, Wisconsin, and the Topps Corporation of Brooklyn, New York, for helping me in my efforts to examine their archived materials and annual corporate reports.

A growing number of cultural studies books that have appeared recently have reserved a special portion of their acknowledgments for George Lipsitz. This book is no exception. In fact, in this case he deserves such attention not only for the immense impact he has had on my own intellectual perspectives, but also for the remarkable patience and faith he has displayed toward this book throughout the almost comic pitfalls that have accompanied its journey to eventual publication. Review comments by Stanley Aronowitz, Lynn Spigel, and anonymous readers were extremely helpful in helping me revise my manuscript. Biodun Iginla, Janaki Bakhle, and Elizabeth Knoll Stomberg at the University of Minnesota Press have also been valuable guides through the publication process. Barbara McDonald at Dickinson College transcribed a number of interviews that I conducted and have drawn from in this book, and aided me with the preparation of my manuscript. The copyediting by Tammy Zambo was also extremely helpful.

My parents, Maxine Bloom and Sidney Bloom, have been supportive with their love and encouragement. Lois Farrell and Jim Farrell also have helped sustain me with their warmth and good humor. Jim Bloom, Kirby Farrell, Laura Farrell, Ann Midgley, and Patrick Midgley have all been sympathetic family members who have spurred me on to the completion of this project.

Finally, I would especially like to thank Amy Farrell, Catherine Ann Farrell Bloom, and Nicholas Farrell Bloom. Amy has been my partner for the past eleven years. She has read every draft of this book and helped me revise it, and she has given me intellectual guidance, spiritual inspiration, and love. Together we have built a life of mutual respect that I am lucky to have. Our son, Nicholas, was not even born when I began working on this book. Now he is in kindergarten and has become an avid sports fan. I dedicate this book to him and to our daughter, Catherine, who was born while this book was in press, with the following words of wisdom: in baseball you might want to always end up at home, but life and imagination offer infinite other possibilities.

Introduction

During the late 1980s and early part of 1990, I spent a great deal of time attending baseball card shows in the metropolitan area of a major city in the upper midwestern United States. It was not hard for me to locate a show to attend, as each week I could easily find groups of men and boys, sometimes accompanied by, but almost never in equitable companionship with, women or girls. They would gather for these events at local hockey arenas, gymnasiums, hotel conference rooms, or shopping mall plazas. Many would come wearing sports paraphernalia: baseball hats, sports jackets, windbreakers, T-shirts, and sweats. But none of them would be exerting themselves, at least not physically. Instead they would be slowly walking up and down aisles, looking at binders and tabletop cases, checking computer printouts in their hands, leafing through paperback indexes they carried, and bargaining and trading cardboard objects for money with one another.

This book is a critical examination of an adult male sports fan culture surrounding baseball card collecting, particularly as it developed and flourished from the 1970s through the 1980s. It is also an exploration of what the baseball card collecting hobby meant to a local population of collectors I spent time with in this upper midwestern urban region. But most important, it is a study of sports spectatorship in the contemporary United States and its all-important relationship to male gender identities and masculinity.

1

Of all the observations one could make of baseball card collecting during the 1980s, that white men comprised the core of its population might seem the least noteworthy. One surely would less likely take for granted more sensational aspects of adult collecting: cards selling for prices comparable to the down payment one might make on a new car or even a new house; grown men hoarding boxes of cards in the hope of trading them for a fortune in the future; a major-league umpire being arrested in a California discount store for shoplifting boxes of baseball cards. Yet it is this seemingly insignificant aspect of the hobby that I will focus on, for I think it may be one of the most important. Gender identity is not a simple matter. It is complicated by other identities people hold as workers or as members of races, classes, ethnic groups, and consumer cultures. This holds true for white men as much as it does for anyone else. Oversimplifying their multifaceted subject positions means missing out on important aspects of gender relations that affect everybody. Not recognizing the contradictions even white men face in constituting their identities only reestablishes both whiteness and masculinity as cultural norms, and repositions "other" identities as culturally marginal.

There is nothing inherently white and male about baseball cards, the game of baseball itself, or sports spectatorship. Cultural practices such as sports are established and understood by people who create them according to their own idealized images, which have themselves been passed down over time, changed again and again to mediate historical experiences more effectively, and struggled over because of the contradictory meanings they embody. This critical study of adult baseball card collecting is less a reflection upon the value of cardboard objects than an introduction to the values of a culture and a people that have made significant little pictures of baseball players sold with bubble gum, and the sport those images depict.

Baseball Cards, Media, and Consumer Culture

For my purposes, baseball cards are important primarily because a relatively large segment of the U.S. population feels passionately about them. But I have also discovered that cards provide an extremely provocative viewpoint from which to examine historically both mass media and sports in the United States. They have introduced a number of children, most often boys, to sports spectatorship, and over the course of a century they have become central to the interpersonal relationships of a great many preadolescent boys.

Baseball cards have existed almost since the beginning of the organized professional game. They are, by definition, an extension of sports spectatorship, used by manufacturers of consumer goods to attract "market segments," in the process creating more fans of sports. Tobacco companies during the 1880s were the first to produce and distribute baseball cards to mass audiences, using them as an advertising mechanism to sell their product as their industry became mechanized and sought new markets to avoid overproduction. These first cards were smaller than contemporary ones (about 1¾ inches by 2¾ inches) and most often contained advertisements rather than statistics or trivia on their backs. Cards produced by the Allen and Ginter Tobacco Company or the Goodwin Tobacco Company during this time period picture players as serious men; they wore perfectly pressed uniforms, sometimes with a necktie, and almost never smiled. Goodwin's cards were black-and-white photographs often showing players posing in "action" positions, such as swinging a bat, fielding a ball, or sliding into a base. Each photo was carefully staged. The photographer, for example, would hang a baseball by a thin string and ask a player to reach for it as if he were going to catch it at first base or in the outfield.

It was not until after World War I that companies would package baseball cards with products such as candy, gum, caramels, or cookies, thereby marketing products directly to children. Like other emerging forms of commercial culture during this time period (popular music, movies, and pulp fiction), baseball cards became an increasingly important aspect of children's lives during the twentieth century, a commercial intervention into preadolescent play during an era in which child labor laws, industrial mechanization, and mandatory schooling all extended childhood and made play an increasingly central aspect of children's lives (Aronowitz 1973, 72–74).

During the 1930s the Goudey Gum Company first used baseball cards to market bubble gum to youths. Its cards presented baseball as wholesome and patriotic while at the same time embodying the "innocent" fun of boyish play. Some contained biographies on the backs signed as if star players such as Lou Gehrig or Chuck Klein had written them. Others were photos of players' heads superimposed atop skinny cartoon bodies. They were sold with coupons that children could send back, allowing them to join a fan club or obtain baseball equipment. By the end of the decade, gum companies increasingly associated baseball cards with patriotic symbols, selling their product wrapped in red, white, and blue paper, evoking images of baseball as the "national pastime."

After World War II, companies regularly produced and sold yearly sets of baseball cards to children for the first time. Beginning in 1948, the Bowman Corporation began printing and selling annual sets of cards with bubble gum each summer. In 1952 the Topps Corporation of Brooklyn, New York, challenged Bowman with a now famous 407-card set. By this time baseball card collecting had already become one of the most popular hobbies among boys in the United States.

Topps eventually was able to maneuver Bowman out of the baseball card market, buying out the company and maintaining a monopoly over baseball card production until the early 1980s. Cards produced after World War II were not used to sell another product but were sold as products in and of themselves. What had once been an advertising mechanism had now become an elaborately crafted form of entertainment. In a space smaller than a postcard, they contained not only photographs but also a wide range of information: a player's throwing, batting, and fielding positions, his team, hometown, and hair and eye color.[1]

Baseball cards have been, all at once, commercial artifacts, forms of visual media, advertising mechanisms, popular art, and objects of exchange. And, most recently, they have become icons for an idealized image of *all* American boyhood, which is to say an image of a specifically white, early post–World War II, middle-class boyhood made universal, transcendent, and mythic. They may not have shaken the planet like rock and roll or revolutionized cultural discourse like television, but in a world transformed by such entertainment bombshells, baseball cards have provided an important level of mediation through which both boys and girls in the United States have experienced sports as spectators and as gendered subjects.

Baseball Cards and Nostalgia during the 1980s

It is the nostalgia, however, that has been historically represented both on baseball cards and by baseball card collectors, that receives the greatest amount of treatment in this volume. The decade of the 1980s might be seen as a watershed for baseball nostalgia. Popular entertainment was filled with representations of baseball's history that had a peculiar "retro" quality, what film critic Viveca Gretton has called a feeling of "pastness" (1990).

Hollywood films such as *The Natural, Eight Men Out,* and perhaps most prominently *Field of Dreams* very self-consciously celebrated baseball as an icon of the American past, a constant, mythic American tradition that has survived unchanged against the alienating transformations of U.S. history. Major publishers released books by celebrated authors such as W. P. Kinsella and Roger Angell, media personalities such as George Will, and the late baseball commissioner A. Bartlett Giamatti, all of which glorified — sometimes almost to the level of self-parody — the game of baseball as a symbol of transcendent meaning (Angell 1984; Giamatti 1990; Kinsella 1982; Will 1990). Many teams in the major leagues cast aside their flamboyant 1970s softball-style uniforms for ones that resembled flannel outfits worn during the 1950s, even though teams such as the Minnesota Twins and San Francisco Giants created entirely new team logos in the process. By the end of the decade, the Baltimore Orioles had abandoned their old ballpark for a new one that was built to *seem* old, and the Cleveland Indians, Colorado Rockies, and Texas Rangers had drawn up plans to do the same thing.

Nostalgia is nothing new to baseball. However, the powerful ways in which it was resurrected during the 1980s reveal a great deal about the contours of gender, race, and class in the United States during the late twentieth century. Baseball fiction writer W. P. Kinsella illustrates this in his 1982 novel *Shoeless Joe* (the book upon which the 1989 film *Field of Dreams* was based). Early in the book, the story's protagonist, Ray Kinsella, is driven by the spirit of Shoeless Joe Jackson to build a baseball diamond in a cornfield that he farms. Eventually, he decides to leave behind his wife, daughter, and financially troubled farm to pursue a baseball odyssey. His first stop is Chicago, where he attends a White Sox game at the old Comiskey Park on the city's South Side:

> It is unwise for a white person to walk through South Chicago, but
> I do anyway. The Projects are chill, sand-colored apartments,
> twelve to fifteen stories high, looking like giant bricks stabbed into
> the ground. I am totally out of place. I glow like a piece of
> phosphorous on a pitch-black night. Pedestrians' heads turn after

me. I feel the stolid stares of drivers as large cars zipper past. A beer can rolls ominously down the gutter, its source of locomotion invisible. The skeletal remains of automobiles litter the parking lots behind apartments. (38)

Two young African American women lie to Kinsella as he walks to the game, telling him that there are some people ready to mug him up the street. When he gets to the ballpark, he describes it as "bleak and raw" on this cold, rainy spring day (40). His concern is not for those who have to live in the frightening and impersonal projects he describes, but rather with his own sense of being out of place. Even "a lone black woman, conspicuously pregnant" who stands at a bus stop is only a metaphor to the protagonist, not a real person toward whom one might feel compassion or empathy. Her gender, poverty, and race, as with the two women who warn Kinsella about the mugger, all represent minority life (and urban public space more generally), as pathological, untrustworthy, and threatening. The neighborhood around the ballpark encroaches upon, and has contaminated, the once pastoral and pure space of the baseball stadium.

Kinsella's description of the neighborhood surrounding Comiskey Park during the early 1980s is loaded with fears and stereotypes that have been particularly harmful to African Americans. Yet there is an equally important subtext in this passage related to urban decline. One senses that Comiskey was at one time a ballpark someone like Kinsella could walk to, through a neighborhood where it would not have been "unwise" for a "white person" to have walked.

In fact, the neighborhood surrounding that ballpark did transform dramatically after World War II. Highway construction and urban renewal eliminated existing housing and replaced it with the infamous and substandard housing projects that Kinsella describes. At the same time, African Americans migrated to the South Side of Chicago in huge numbers. As white flight from the city to the suburbs decreased the white population, the black population of Chicago increased, from 14 percent in 1950 to 33 percent in 1970. Because of housing discrimination, however, these new residents faced extreme overcrowding once in the city. In 1960, African Americans were 23 percent of Chicago's population but occupied only 4 percent of its housing (Trotter 1991).

It is not necessarily inappropriate for Kinsella to have painted a depressing picture, therefore, of the South Side. In fact, it is one that speaks to the historical conditions created by suburbanization, discrimination, redlining, freeway construction, deindustrialization, and urban renewal. By the early 1980s such developments had impoverished a number of urban centers and gutted once-vibrant city neighborhoods. Yet by offering the nostalgic comfort of baseball as his alternative to the realities of late-twentieth-century U.S. city life, the author makes it seem as if urban problems were created by the nonwhite urban poor. The popularity of his writing during this time period suggests that baseball nostalgia provided a comforting fantasy about the nation's past that spoke very specifically to white men and that responded to the social conditions of the time.

If filmmakers, authors, and stadium architects self-consciously accessed baseball nostalgia to create mythic representations, and if these representations were metaphors for stability among white middle-class men, what did the return to a boyish baseball card collecting hobby mean for those adult males who became involved in it? White middle-class men were the primary constituency that comprised the core of the baseball card collecting hobby, not only in the Upper Midwest but throughout the rest of the United States as well.[2] Collectors addressed their own insecurities about their authority and position as white men in the United States partly through their affinity for baseball cards. However, baseball card collecting, although often nostalgic, is also quite contradictory and not as easily analyzed or interpreted as are produced images.

This is why the core of this book is an ethnographic account of a local fan culture surrounding baseball card collecting. As Henry Jenkins has argued, audiences do many different things with the culture that is commercially produced for them, and the study of fans opens up new possibilities for understanding how people make meaning from mass-cultural forms. Yet the study of audiences also creates ethnographic problems. One cannot think of fans as an autonomous, coherent group. Instead, ethnographers who study media audiences must see how those audiences are linked to multiple identities and to innumerable cultures outside their fan culture; how they exist at specific historic moments and in specific places; and how they are created and maintained through elaborate systems of cultural production (Jenkins 1992, 3).

This book is not a definitive account of sports spectatorship, of the baseball card hobby, or even of a small community of collectors.

It is, however, an account of how members of a group of sports fans are coherently linked by some commonly understood cultural meanings that they associate with baseball cards and with sports. The kind of study I provide here is possible only because of innovative trends in the field of anthropology over the past decades, particularly with regard to the use of ethnography. My local observations of middle-class male American sports fans are shaped in large part by what George Marcus and Michael Fischer call "repatriated ethnography," or the use of ethnographic fieldwork methods to study cultures most familiar to a researcher. Marcus and Fischer write that such methods can "defamiliarize" people with their "taken-for-granted" surroundings and allow researchers critically to understand the dynamics of their own cultures. Marcus and Fischer encourage ethnographers to disrupt common sense, do "the unexpected," and place "familiar objects in unfamiliar, or even shocking, contexts." In particular, they see great possibilities in ethnographers looking beyond traditional anthropological categories or topics, and urge researchers to pay attention instead to popular culture and, "somewhat more tentatively," "mainstream middle-class life" (1986, 136–53).

When I first encountered Marcus and Fischer's writings as a graduate student, I was eagerly (and not tentatively) taken by their suggestion to study mass media and middle-class life ethnographically. As I have moved ever more cautiously through this project over the years, I have become increasingly committed to the importance of doing this kind of work. Unlike other ethnographic studies of subcultures, mine examines a group that draws its constituency from mainstream, middle-class American life. There is, of course, a danger in studying white middle-class men. In media marketing research and political polling, this demographic group is often considered the norm, their ideas and emotions universally identified with the nation at large. White middle-class men are all too often identified as the "everyman," the "heartbeat of the nation." If the lives of such a population are not examined in their historical and situational contexts, it might be easy to reaffirm their "mainstream" status rather than to throw it under a critical light. Yet this is not what happened for me during my research. In fact, the very process of examining a "mainstream" population's affinity for everyday objects has been, for me, a profound experience in what Marcus and Fischer call "defamiliarization," in understanding how cultural meanings with important social implications are defined and struggled with in the contexts of people's daily lives. I am a white, middle-class, heterosexually identified man. I am also a baseball fan (although I do not collect baseball cards), and a more general sports fan as well. Such information is important for readers to know, for I am not an outsider looking in, and I have a particularly large stake in the things about which I write. I say this in part to dispel any sense that I am a neutral observer, for recent movements in ethnography have sufficiently unmasked the ideal of ethnographic impartiality and distance (see Clifford and Marcus 1986). Moreover, I want readers to know that I feel passionate about this topic — that I take fandom seriously, even if what I have learned about it does not always make me happy.

Baseball cards, sports fandom, and sports were all a part of my boyhood and are part of my gendered identity as an adult. However, by what I now consider to be a lucky freak of nature, I never was a particularly gifted athlete. My experiences with most sports at almost all stages of my life have been as a spectator, and my active participation has been relegated to the sandlots. I consider this lucky because I think it has helped me gain a good understanding of how sports mean many different things to audiences, what fans do with the sports they watch, and how the meanings of popular athletics can be negotiated and contested within the informal rules of sandlot games and within the fantasies and emotions of spectators.

As a fan, I am perhaps also less inclined than some to distinguish sports as more "real" than other forms of entertainment that are "fiction." What, after all, is more unreal than an event such as the Super Bowl: the spectacle of media noise and all-encompassing commercial endorsement; the price of tickets and fabulous display of wealth; the larger-than-life uniforms that turn the human body into a robotlike machine; the high-tech, cast-of-thousands halftime shows; and even the steroid-induced strength of the athletes themselves? In fact, I think my fan identity has allowed me to understand sports as a part of an intertextual entertainment world that is no more and no less "real" for its audiences than soap operas or romance novels are for theirs.

Because of this background, I hope to interject the discussion of athletics into larger intellectual conversations about popular culture in the United States that have evolved over the past twenty years or so but that have largely overlooked sports as a serious topic of inquiry. Sports are an extremely high-profile aspect of entertainment culture, a formidable component of community life, and an inescapable aspect of nearly every American's formal education. Athletics has become meaningful in the United States through its associations with gender, race, money, success, and competition. The inquiry of sports as a serious intellectual pursuit not only addresses issues important to both citizens and cultural scholars but also enlightens the ways in which such issues are a part of people's lived experiences and daily lives. The study of sports audiences allows those interested in popular culture scholarship to broaden their understanding of male gender identities, opening the field to the critical examination of peculiarly male fan cultures. Furthermore, to include sports as forms of entertainment, and audiences as members of fan cultures, is to move away from elevating sports to a status of "real" and from thereby implying that they are more important than other, more female-dominated fan cultures. I hope not only to disabuse readers about the privileged status of sports but also to present more complicated understandings of the way male gender identities are popularly expressed through sports fandom.

Adult baseball card collecting sheds important light upon the conflicting ways in which sports spectatorship itself speaks to the gendered memories and identities of male audience members. For the collectors I spoke with, professional baseball and most other spectator sports provided an important and very real context for the establishment of all-male interpersonal relationships in childhood. As Michael Oriard (1984) discusses, the very act of a boy watching a sport such as football with his father creates a kind of bond that constitutes both community and heroic action as exclusively male. However, the interview subjects' return to a boyhood hobby oriented their gender identities in two very different directions. On the one hand, baseball cards recalled the heroism of men whom the boys admired and who excelled in competition, displayed grace under pressure, and exhibited manly strength. At the same time, however, baseball cards also evoked a longing for boyhood itself, a desire to recapture a feeling of innocence and playfulness popularly associated with white middle-class boys and baseball.

This latter sentiment complicates a number of theoretical approaches to sports, masculinity, and gender relations. Most contemporary scholars who have critically studied male understandings of athletics have focused on how sports represent male dominance through demonstrations of physical strength and power (Bryson 1987; Messner 1988; Whitson 1990). Others have also analyzed how male sports often ritually symbolize militaristic and domineering forms of masculine competition (Bray 1983; Foley 1989; Sabo and Runfola 1980). Such perspectives are not necessarily incorrect, but they are somewhat incomplete, for they do not really address the all-important commercially mediated contexts of sports spectatorship in the United States, which, like other forms of popular entertainment, embodies a number of contradictions, even with regard to gender.

Early in my own work it became hard for me to think of grown men's return to a childhood hobby as an expression of an aggressive and tough masculine persona (although, as I will point out, many of the ways in which collectors operated within their hobby did mirror aspects of masculine competition). In fact, to see sports and sports fandom as unproblematically symbolic of manliness is to miss their historical relationship to some hotly contested ideas about gender. In 1919, Thorstein Veblen, for example, provided a sharp critique of sports spectatorship in *The Theory of the Leisure Class*, writing that fandom reflected the decadence of a consumer, or "leisure," class of men. Rather than seeing sports spectatorship as symbolically validating male authority, Veblen understood male spectators as doing the opposite. He argued there was nothing publicly productive, and therefore manly, about cheering on a sports team. Rather, he viewed spectators as unproductive consumers of the games they watched for pleasure, which themselves promoted both an animalistic, predatory ethos and a boyish passivity: "It is perhaps truer, or at least more evident, as regards sports than as regards the other expressions of predatory emulation already spoken of, that the temperament which inclines men to them is essentially a boyish temperament" (255–56).

According to Veblen, those who celebrated sports as morally productive forms of male recreation were really only rationalizing their own perverse decadence to make fandom seem productive and socially beneficial. Veblen's criticism of sports, to a large extent echoed later in the century by Christopher Lasch (1978), implicitly upheld notions of male authority central to a patriarchal culture. However, Veblen's opinions about sports also provide one illustration of how sports fandom in the United States has long embodied a complex set of tensions between manhood and boyhood.

In the time since Veblen wrote his essay, the United States has transformed from a nation with one class of people who consumed a great deal, to a society fundamentally built on leisure, entertainment, and consumption. The men I observed collecting baseball cards were precisely those whom Veblen would have identified as belonging to a class of productive "common men" whose virtue contrasted with the decadence of the leisure class. But during the contemporary era they have become consumers themselves, in this case sports fans who have come to express their understanding of self not primarily through their communities nor through their work, but most passionately through the athletic contests they watch and experience as sports fans, and through the commercial objects they purchase. Veblen's analysis serves as a reminder that for such spectators, sports are meaningful as something make-believe and symbolic. If those who compete successfully in sports must have skill and power, fans who enjoy sports must understand athletics as playful fantasy. The popular affinity for baseball cards demonstrated by adult men suggests that nostalgic fantasies surrounding boyhood are in fact an important way in which male spectators identify with the sports they watch.

However, I also observed collectors engaging in forms of behavior that contradicted their ability to appreciate sports nostalgically through baseball cards. The very act of collecting—sorting, ordering, and arranging cards; keeping them in perfect condition; and conducting painstaking searches to complete sets—detached these objects from the contexts in which they had originally been meaningful to collectors. Instead, they became components guided by a larger set of what Susan Stewart has called "principles of organization." Stewart argues that collections actually represent a negation of nostalgia rather than an expression of it. Any unique characteristic that a collected object might have gets washed away as it becomes another unit within a serial. As with money, the usefulness of collected objects is entirely replaced by their value as objects of exchange. For Stewart this is particularly true for objects such as beer cans, old clothing, political buttons, and other items she calls ephemera. She argues that collections of such items represent "the ultimate form of consumerism" in the fascination with novelty and fashion that they evoke (1984, 151–68).

The adults I observed collected vintage baseball cards in this manner, and their practices frequently existed in tension with baseball nostalgia. Men within the hobby collected methodically, avoiding the trading games they often remembered playing as children. Their cards were meaningful primarily as constituents within a serial, or a "set." This made it hard for hobbyists to assess the emotional value of their cards; instead they conflated all discussions of an object's worth with the rhetoric of economic exchange, of cold, hard currency. Yet collectors I interviewed often expressed bewilderment at this process, discussing how the inflated prices for cards listed in price guides had become inconceivable. As one man put it during an interview, "There's no value in cardboard."

Rather than completely emptying cards of meaning, however, as Stewart's analysis of collecting suggests, baseball card collecting exhibits some contradictions central to a consumer culture that simultaneously detaches people from history and promises the fulfillment of memory through consumer products and commercial entertainment. Baseball cards were indeed meaningful as objects to collectors, because they were remembered as—and had been, in fact—a part of the social world that many men knew as boys and for which they often expressed a sense of reverence. It is just as important to understand collectors' sentiments as it is to recognize the trivialized and commodified character of their actual collections. Although baseball cards may not ultimately bring collectors the stability they seek, the nostalgia for innocence located in symbols of white middle-class boyhood reveals a great deal about cultural expressions of masculinity and their relationship to those of whiteness within contemporary structures of patriarchy and racism.

I have organized this book to provide an understanding of how baseball cards and sports spectatorship can become meaningful through a commodified culture industry; through collectors' active processes; and within the historical, institutional, and social contexts in which baseball cards have been produced and consumed. Chapter 1 provides an introduction to the institutional context of the boom in baseball card collecting in the United States during the 1980s. Nostalgic expressions may have emerged organically from the experiences and positions of white men, but nostalgia has also represented a marketing opportunity that has been very quickly seized upon by baseball card manufacturers. What is more, the saturation of the sports card market by the end of the 1980s ironically began to undermine the very foundations upon which collecting had been built, threatening to empty cards of all meaning but their exchange value. The tensions created by a commercial culture industry demonstrate that collectors feel deep and conflicting emotions that lie beneath the better-publicized surface of greed within the baseball card collecting "market."

Chapter 2 is an introduction to the local hobby I observed as an ethnographic researcher in the Upper Midwest between 1988 and 1990. I explore the gender dynamics of the collecting public and the relationship of these dynamics to issues of race and class within the most public aspects of baseball card collecting. My observations illustrate some of the conflicting sentiments between boyhood and manhood, as well as between cooperation and competition, that collectors managed within their hobby. In addition, I discuss how tensions concerning gender and race, and particularly concerning the commodified status of baseball cards, undermined the fantasies of order and coherence popularly symbolized through baseball nostalgia and articulated through collecting itself.

In chapter 3, I explore the conflicts embodied within the hobby's most common practice: set collecting. As collectors attempted to piece together ordered, coherent sets of cards, they engaged in behavior very much like that Stewart describes. But they also maintained nostalgic attachments, both to their cards and to sports spectatorship more generally, that spoke to a longing for their preadolescent past.

Chapter 4 retrospectively documents the emergence of the adult baseball card collecting hobby during the 1970s among a generation of men who collected these objects in their youth, and the implications of their nostalgia for the politics of gender and race. These men often expressed a feeling of defensive struggle with the symbolic meaning of baseball. They faced issues surrounding the monetary value of cards very early, and they expressed a feeling that baseball cards and baseball itself were changing in ways they did not like. Their nostalgia is important, for it emerged at a moment in history when advances in civil rights, together with economic stagnation, had encroached upon the economic and social entitlements that white men had enjoyed over the previous twenty-five years. As important, baseball's own mythic renderings of gender, race, and national identity had also become increasingly challenged within popular representations of the game and ignored by promoters of major-league baseball itself.

In my concluding chapter I explore the significance of this nostalgia, asking why a longing for boyhood and male bonding would be important to the gender dynamics of contemporary sports spectatorship in the United States, and examining the implications of this same desire. I argue that the popularization of baseball nostalgia throughout the past one hundred years illustrates not only conflicting ways of appreciating sports but also the conflicting positions men often feel themselves assuming within modern structures of patriarchal social relations. The nostalgia I observed among men within baseball card collecting represents a particularly troubling reaction to whatever "crisis" in masculinity men may currently feel themselves facing. For many, the hobby promises to provide a sense of connection to others, but one based upon the exclusion and distancing of men from women. More often than it fulfills its social possibilities, it tends to deliver a frightening sense of loneliness and fragmentation from communities and from the past.

Throughout these chapters I argue that male sports spectatorship is the product of numerous cultural expressions, despite its many commercial forms. Even though adult male baseball card collecting reveals a number of important insights into male sports audiences, it is only one such expression. Sports have also been a part of and have spoken to the conflicting positions that nearly every class and category of men and women in the modern United States has defended, managed, or challenged. To understand what baseball card collecting can reveal about the institution of sports in the United States, I first look at the growth of a baseball card collecting industry during the 1980s and the tensions that industry created among collectors across the United States.

1

The Baseball Card Industry

Between 1975 and 1980, the baseball card collecting hobby among adults grew rapidly in the United States. *Baseball Card Boom* magazine asserts that "serious" collectors increased from 4,000 to 250,000 during this time period, making baseball card collecting the fourth largest hobby in the nation. The number of annual shows increased as well, from twenty to six hundred. Over the next ten years, the hobby continued to grow, involving between 3 million and 4 million people by 1989 (Larson 1990). In 1979, James Beckett and Dennis Eckes published the first *Sports Americana Baseball Card Price Guide*, one of the most important developments in the growing popularity of baseball card dealing and collecting. As the first nationally distributed, widely read listing of baseball card prices in the hobby, it provided a public record of the money many adult men were making selling their baseball cards and prompted many not previously interested in collecting to become involved.[1]

In addition to the publication of Beckett and Eckes's price guide, the publication of the hobby's most popular journal, *Sports Collectors Digest (SCD)*, changed dramatically in ways that helped to market the hobby to a mass audience. In 1981, John Stommen, a private publisher from Milan, Michigan, sold *SCD* to Krause Publications of Iola, Wisconsin, a private corporation that produced coin and automobile collecting magazines. Encouraged by Bob Lemke, an editor who worked at Krause, to provide an additional publication to supplement its new newsstand monthly, *Baseball Cards* magazine, Krause offered Stommen a flat fee to purchase *SCD*. Although the publication still accepted unsolicited articles, Krause hired a professional editorial staff and professional full-time writers, some of whom had previously worked as professional sports journalists (Ellingboe 1990).

Krause's publishing apparatus allowed for expanded printing and distribution capabilities that Stommen alone could not afford. In his first editorial to readers, Lemke guaranteed that Krause would never miss a mailing deadline. In addition, Krause changed the format of *SCD*, increasing the size of the publication (from 7¾ by 10½ to 8½ by 11 inches) and using more sophisticated color graphics (Lemke 1981). With the ability to expand production rapidly, the circulation of both *Baseball Cards* and *SCD* increased as well. Immediately following the *SCD* buyout, *Baseball Cards* had a circulation of 30,000 (Ellingboe 1990). By the end of the 1980s, it would become Krause's largest-circulation magazine, with more than 250,000 issues printed per month. The circulation of *SCD* also jumped, from 6,000 in 1980 to 50,000 in 1989. In addition, in 1987, Krause increased its frequency of publication from biweekly to weekly. By the end of the decade, it was also selling new publications, such as an annual price guide (to compete with Beckett and Eckes's), magazines such as the *Baseball Card Price Guide Monthly* and *Baseball Card Boom,* and a newspaper bought from its original publisher in 1986, *Baseball Card News* (Krause Publications 1989).

Perhaps the most important changes that helped to promote baseball card collecting among adult men in the 1980s, however, took place within the baseball card manufacturing industry itself. Within the changing composition of this industry, the collecting of new cards and sets was promoted to adults along with the vintage cards that were sold or traded among dealers and collectors. In 1975 the Fleer Corporation of Philadelphia, which manufactured candy and gum products and had periodically produced baseball, football, and other sports cards in the 1960s, filed an antitrust suit against Topps in federal district court. Fleer alleged that the exclusive contracts Topps signed with players, major-league baseball, and the Major League Baseball Players Association constituted a restraint of trade. In the late summer of 1980, Judge Clarence Newcomer ruled in favor of Fleer. The ruling opened the door for Fleer and a third company, Donruss of Memphis, Tennessee (then a wholly owned subsidiary of General Mills), to produce complete baseball card sets for the 1981 season. Although Fleer received damages of only $3 million (it had asked for $17.8 million), its new set was very successful. One year later, Newcomer's decision was overruled in the United States Circuit Court of Appeals. However, the new ruling gave Topps only the exclusive right to market cards with a confection. Fleer and Donruss maintained the licensing agreements they had worked out with major-league baseball and the players union, and simply sold their cards without gum (Taylor 1981; 1990).

In addition to sets produced by these major card manufacturers, small regional or promotional sets blossomed in the 1980s. Often these were distributed by local police departments, major-league teams, retailers, or food companies. In the late 1970s there was only a handful of such sets, such as the Los Angeles and San Francisco Police Department sets distributed through the Dodgers and Giants, or the Kellogg's cereal sets distributed throughout the decade with boxes of various products sold by the company. By the end of the 1980s, there were three baseball police department sets, various Smokey Bear sets to promote fire safety, and sets sold to promote J. C. Penney, Kmart, Burger King, McDonald's, Ralston Purina, Mother's Cookies, and other companies selling bread, sausage, beef jerky, iced tea, cereal, soda, potato chips, and oatmeal. Most of these sets featured only a local team or all-star players, and all were used to promote some sponsoring company or organization. Often a company such as Topps would actually produce these cards under a joint agreement with the sponsoring organization (Kiefer 1990b).[2]

By the end of the 1980s, major-league baseball recognized the potential of marketing baseball cards to a wide range of fans and had signed licensing agreements with two more baseball card companies. Each of the two new companies selling cards in the late 1980s put out "high-end products" aimed to include both child and adult male consumers, featuring expanded statistics, high-quality "action" photography, and attractive color graphics. The first company, Score, arose from three parent companies: Optigraphics of Grand Prairie, Texas; Armurol, a distribution subsidiary of Wrigley Gum; and Major League Marketing. After producing a three-dimensional set for children in 1986 and 1987, Score came out with its regular set, distributed in 1988. In addition to high-quality graphics, each card featured biographical paragraphs written by Les Woodcock, the first editor of *Sports Illustrated* (Ambrosius 1990b). In 1989 an Orange County, California, company called Upper Deck began distributing what it bragged was the "BMW" of baseball cards. In addition to high-quality color photos on the front and back of each card, as well as high-bond cardboard and silver foil shrink-wrapped packaging, Upper Deck cards featured a hologram to "prevent" counterfeiting. They were marketed largely to the expanded adult collectors' market, originally selling for eighty-nine cents per pack in 1990, nearly twice the price for a pack of cards from any of the other four card companies (Ambrosius 1990c; Landsbaum 1990).

In addition to the increase in direct marketing by baseball card companies, cable television home-shopping channels became a forum for baseball card and memorabilia auctions during the late 1980s and early 1990s. Shopping networks such as QVC, as well as regional cable sports channels, began to air regularly televised sales of collectors' merchandise, such as cards, autographed balls, and uniforms. With all of this hype, it is not hard to recognize the significance of commercial factors in seeding the popularity of baseball card collecting around the United States during the 1980s. Companies such as Topps, the oldest producer of baseball cards, benefited greatly from the emergence of adult collecting as a major hobby and increasingly took an active role in promoting it over the course of the decade. Even though Topps had fought competition from other baseball card producers during the 1970s, its profits over the next ten years demonstrate that it benefited greatly from the increased adult consumption that developed as new companies' sets flooded the market. In addition, as companies have expanded their sales of cards to include an ever greater variety of sports outside of baseball, the new cards have, in effect, served as advertisements promoting the adult hobby, thus bringing the companies greater revenues.

Scholars Lisa Lewis and David Marc have each demonstrated how producers of commercial entertainment attempt to garner large audiences in part by dividing populations into specific demographic groups and attempting to capture a particular audience (Lewis 1990, 15; Marc 1984). Since it was founded in 1938 by Abram Shorin, Ira Shorin, Philip Shorin, and Joseph Shorin, Topps has aimed to sell a wide variety of products to a six- to twelve-year-old market. Unlike other media distribution outlets, however, Topps initially produced other consumer commodities. Its first product was Bazooka bubble gum, and Topps has historically seen itself as primarily a producer of gum and confectionery products. Soon after it incorporated in 1947, the company expanded into baseball card production, which eventually led to its printing trading cards and collectibles associated with other sports and forms of entertainment, including popular music, motion pictures, and television programs. In the 1950s Topps obtained licenses to print Hopalong Cassidy and Elvis Presley cards, and in the 1970s and 1980s produced cards featuring, among other subjects, the Beatles, *Star Wars, Charlie's Angels,* and *E. T.* In addition, Topps has printed novelty cards and stickers, such as its "Mars Attacks" card set in the early 1960s, its mid-1980s "Garbage Pail Kids" stickers, and its "Wacky Packages" stickers that feature satirical ads for everyday consumer goods (e.g., "Crust" toothpaste and "Log Cave-In" pancake syrup) (Topps Corporation 1990). As evidenced by the level of humor on these stickers, all of these products have been designed to attract a preadolescent market.

Yet Topps has also long recognized children as a particularly unstable market that has tended to change rapidly and whose consumer tastes have rarely been constant (Jakubovics 1989). Maintaining consumer interest always has been a concern for Topps, because it has seen itself as marketing, to a great extent, "fad" products in competition not only with other trading card companies or candy and gum producers, "but also with snack food products, small toys, comic books, and other low-priced products appealing to children" (Topps Corporation 1990, 9). Sales of baseball cards to adult collectors have opened up a whole new arena of competition for Topps in which upstart companies have, compared to Topps, fewer resources (9).

The early to mid-1980s were volatile years for Topps. In both 1980 and 1981, its net sales dropped, after a decade and a half of near constant growth. In 1984 Topps was obtained in a $94 million leveraged buyout led by Forstman Little and Co., an investment firm that included ten members of Topps management. The syndicate privatized the company that same year (Will Topps Offer 1989; Topps Holder Group 1988). Yet between 1981 and 1990, Topps's net sales grew every year except 1986 (when a product associated with Bazooka bubble gum failed) (Topps Company, Inc. 1987). Between 1986 and 1990, net sales increased dramatically from $73,473,000 to $246,399,000. During this same time period, sales of sports cards increased from $30,231,000 to $166,109,000. Net sales for sports picture cards in 1990 alone nearly exceeded the net sales for the entire company only two years earlier. In addition, despite increased revenue from candy, gum, and other entertainment cards, the percentage of net sales attributable to sports picture cards rose from 39 percent in 1985 to 67 percent in 1990 (Topps Corporation 1972–1986; 1990).

For candy and gum companies such as Topps, the sale of picture products is especially important. Not only do products such as baseball cards keep the company name in front of consumers, but they also retain a higher margin of profit than other products produced by the company. Thus Topps had a keen interest in promoting baseball card collecting and investing among adults. After the success of its 1986 sports cards (ending in fiscal year 1987), Topps wrote in its corporate report,

> [S]ales of such traditional products as baseball picture cards can...
> be significantly impacted by changing consumer tastes and
> interests. Sales of baseball and other sports products almost
> doubled in fiscal 1987 from fiscal 1986, partially as a result of
> increased consumer interest in the investment and collectible value
> of cards. (Topps Company, Inc. 1987, 5)

As a consequence, Topps extended its season for the release of cards and improved distribution by increasing the frequency and size of deliveries to "convenience and variety stores, mass merchandisers and toy outlets." In addition, it increased wholesale distribution to "a growing number of hobby card dealers" (11).

By 1989 the increased sales in sports products had become a major focus of the company. "Increased consumer interest in baseball cards, extension of the Company's product line, increased distribution to supermarkets, wholesale clubs and other mass merchandisers, and, to a lesser extent, price increases and increased manufacturing capacity" all contributed to the rise in sales. In other words, by 1989, Topps felt it could count on adult consumers to provide a steady market, and it hit that market heavily. Seeing adult dealers as major wholesale buyers, Topps introduced "Big Baseball" cards, collectible baseball coins, and a card-collecting kit to its lists of merchandised items (Topps Company, Inc. 1989, 9).

By 1990, Topps had introduced a new line of baseball cards with the Bowman brand label it had bought thirty-four years earlier, clearly creating a hook for the nostalgic impulses of its adult market. In addition, it began *Topps Magazine,* a glossy quarterly publication with articles about baseball and, of course, ads for Topps products (Topps: Baseball Bubble-Gum Maker 1989; Rothenberg 1989, C5[n]). Topps promoted its products aggressively to dealers and hobby shops around the country. In its 1990 annual report to the Securities and Exchange Commission, Topps wrote:

> Based on trade literature and increased sales to hobby dealers, the Company believes that sales of collectible picture products, primarily sports, to adults have been growing in recent years, and although it is the leading marketer of collectible picture products and attempts to capitalize on that status in its marketing, it competes for the attention of the adult market with other hobby collectible products. The Company competes in the collectible picture card market by designing products which it believes will especially appeal to adult collectors, in addition to children, and by mailing promotional literature relating to such products to wholesale and retail hobby and collectible product dealers throughout the United States. (Topps Corporation 1990, 9)

During the 1970s, primarily dealers, collectors, and hobby magazine publishers promoted baseball card collecting among adult men, but the story of Topps illustrates how, by the mid- to late 1980s, baseball card companies were aggressively getting into the act. By 1988, the year before Upper Deck entered the baseball card market, the total net sales of the four companies selling complete baseball card sets exceeded $250 million. Even though the secondary market (which consisted of dealers selling vintage cards) was estimated to be twice as large that year, baseball card companies were taking an ever greater role in defining the hobby (Jannings 1989). In many ways they displaced the older hobbyists who had begun to attend conventions and collect cards on an organized basis during the 1970s. Although Topps began heavily promoting the adult hobby during the 1980s in an effort to seek market stability, its actions actually undermined the metaphorical understandings many adult men associated with their cards, making memories and identities they formulated through these objects confusing and problematic.

Because Topps and the other baseball card companies defined their adult consumers in demographic terms, they had no real understanding of the complex motivations—other than financial speculation in collectible items—that drove men to buy their cards. For example, during the 1990 season Donruss, then a subsidiary of the Leaf candy company, packaged sets made up entirely of "rookie cards," cards marking a star player's first season in major-league baseball.[3] This strategy shows that Donruss had recognized that collectors were investing in rookie cards. In addition, collectors often believed that companies intentionally sold cards with flipped negative images or incorrectly spelled names because of the high value of "error" cards, or cards printed incorrectly, on the secondary market (I Will Swap 1990).

Yet, as Lewis points out, demographic marketing of this kind "may categorize consumers well, but it is less adept at providing information that takes into account their social context." Demographic analysis tends to divide individuals into identities of age, gender, ethnicity, class, and race, but reduces to consumer tastes and preferences the differences that emerge from these identities. Conflicts that arise in all individuals who are defined by multiple identities tend to be washed over by apolitical demographic categories. Lewis writes that demographic marketing in television classifies viewers "in strict consumerist terms, according to features that function more as indeterminate variables than human characteristics" (1990, 21).

By not recognizing the complex motivations that drive adult collectors and the metaphorical relationships between baseball cards and broader social and historical contexts, baseball card companies have evoked a great many tensions. Hobbyists did not always articulate their resentment directly to companies, but tensions rose ever higher as shows and dealers proliferated during the 1980s and as investing in cards for their resale value began to drive up card prices.

Just as companies fueled the growth of the hobby, the expanded circulation of *SCD* created publicity for the growing number of dealers, shops, and shows around the United States. *SCD* has long maintained a listing of baseball card conventions around the country. When it was bought by Krause, it began listing shows by region and, by the end of the decade, by state. Independent dealers or groups of dealers began promoting shows for profit with increasing frequency during the 1980s. Baseball card writer Rusty Morse estimated that the number of shows held in 1987 comprised more than a third of all shows that had been held since 1973. The same was true in 1988 (Butler 1990).

With the expanded opportunities that shows and publications offered to those selling baseball cards, full-time dealers also became more and more common. In the late 1970s only a handful could make a living selling baseball cards and memorabilia. By the end of the decade, thousands of dealers across the country owned card shops and traveled from show to show every year. Perhaps the most famous was Alan Rosen, nicknamed "Mr. Mint." A former New Jersey copy machine salesman, Rosen took out full-page ads in *SCD* in the early 1980s. He claimed to carry a briefcase with $100,000 in hundred-dollar bills, which he said he would use to pay top value for any card to any collector or dealer at any time (Ambrosius 1990a). His ads stated, "No one pays more than 'Mr. Mint,'" and his flamboyance gained him widespread attention and celebration in the popular media. He was featured in an article in *Sports Illustrated* as well as on *Good Morning America* and *Nightline* (Kiefer 1990a). In 1990 the magazine *Business Week Assets* gushed that Rosen cleared $190,000 at a baseball card auction he held on October 19, 1987, the same day that the bottom fell out of the New York Stock Exchange (Garr 1990).

Yet despite his media image as a folk hero of 1980s-style American capitalism, Rosen and other dealers who have made a lot of money selling cards have been widely resented among hobbyists and dealers. Many have seen Rosen's monetary gain as destabilizing their attachment to baseball cards. Even *SCD* editor Tom Mortenson recently told the *Wall Street Journal,* "I felt a little remorse, because the average individual gets priced out of the market." Rosen has responded to such complaints merely by accusing his critics of envy: "It sounds to me like they're jealous. . . . sure we've ruined their hobby, but isn't that what America is all about?" (I Will Swap 1990).

It is important to note that I first heard this quotation from several collectors during formal and informal interviews, indicating that it resonated to some extent with their experiences within the hobby. In the same *Wall Street Journal* article in which Rosen's quotation appeared, veteran collector Lew Lipset was quoted from his self-published monthly newsletter: "We're fixated on money and sports, and cards are just another chance to put them together. . . . try to make a living in this hobby and you'll learn about deceit, unfair business practices, the lack of truth in advertising, price manipulation, collusion, restraint of trade, insider trading, patronage, extortion, payoffs and bribes, plagiarism and, last but not least, hype" (I Will Swap 1990). With the increased attention to the monetary value of cards, theft and fraud became common in the hobby (Thefts 1990; Teens Suspected 1990). Many collectors in the upper midwestern metropolitan area where I focused my research told me that their cards had been stolen at shows or that they had been sold counterfeit or altered cards. One prominent promoter of shows in the area quit collecting after his entire 1962 Topps set was stolen at a show he was promoting. Such stories and experiences undermined the notion that shows warmly evoke a sense of male bonding and solidarity, and instead illustrated how shows could just as powerfully create an atmosphere of public distrust and cynicism.

For many in the hobby, such petty crimes are symptomatic of broader problems that emerged as standards of value became universalized through monetary exchange. For instance, the value of cards was increasingly determined by physical condition in the 1980s. *Beckett's Price Guide* listed prices for cards in "mint," "near mint," and "very good" condition in the front of each volume. By the end of the decade, a former coin dealer by the name of Alan Hager had begun offering a mail-order grading service; collectors could send in their cards and pay a fee to have them assigned a numerical grade on a scale of 1 to 100 (Liscio 1990).

Many came to resent this development as an intrusion into the hobby. One longtime collector whom I interviewed told me that concern over condition had taken over all aspects of the hobby and had virtually ruined it for him. Even those who have written in the pages of the hobby's most widely circulated magazines have expressed ambivalence along these lines. An October 1986 article in *Sports Collectors Digest* warned that coin dealers could soon be attracted to baseball card collecting because of the relatively low price of cards. Predicting that sets would go up in price, the article's author stated, "I expect we are going to see complete sets from the 1950s and 1960s under increasing pressure as many of these coin dealers would remember such era cards from their boyhood days." The article went on to warn:

> The condition is likely to become increasingly important and as anyone who has been involved in coins will attest, it has everything to do with price. A coin in top condition is often worth hundreds of times the value of the same coin that has been widely circulated. . . . Coin dealers believe in quality. They are going to look at a 1952 Topps Eddie Matthews and be more than willing to spend the extra

25

dollars to get a top quality example. . . . a relatively small number of dealers could have a substantial impact. (Green 1986)

This article demonstrates some of the ways money complicated the meaning of adult baseball card collecting. On the one hand, money signified that powerful people with disposable incomes were interested in baseball cards. As the author of the article put it, "I must admit to having some reservations about the entrance of coin dealers into the hobby, but at the same time, it seems flattering that they would find the hobby so interesting." Yet this same writer also characterized baseball hobbyists as having a pure, authentic identity in relation to the cards they collect, and represented coin collectors as a corrupting outside influence. This theme was further reinforced by a cartoon accompanying the article that pictured a greedy, smiling coin dealer, eyes bulging, teeth missing, fumbling with a baseball card. Coins were shown falling out of his hands onto a tabletop stacked with money (Green 1986). What was most at stake in such representations was not the price of cards but the integrity of adult collecting as a "real" site of social activity implicitly based on a sense of male bonding and sports nostalgia, rather than a breeding ground for selfishness and greed.

These same issues of control appeared in 1981 when Krause Publications bought the *Sports Collectors Digest* from John Stommen, who had begun the magazine nearly a decade earlier and had operated it as a relatively informal "fanzine." As Bob Lemke's opening editorial pointed out, the new publisher provided the publication with greater potential audiences but at the same time took a degree of control away from collectors who had built the hobby. The deadline policy that Lemke outlined in the first issue (1981) highlighted this problem:

[The] promised mailing date is our part of the deal — here's yours. All ads, news, columns, features, calendar listings, etc., have to be in our office by noon on the Wednesday before mailing. This means that if you want something to appear in our Oct. 9 issue, we have to have it in hand by noon on Sept. 23. Not "in the mail" but in our hands. Time, tide, and *SCD* wait for no man (or woman).

This policy was a dramatic change from the rather loose deadline policy "enforced" by Stommen. Some readers reacted with hostility to this new corporate structure and to *SCD*'s new management, sometimes writing that they no longer felt a part of the publication. In one of the first issues to appear after the buyout, a reader from Tonswanda, New York, angrily wrote a letter complaining, "Could you ask your columnists to write their columns about collecting? I buy a newspaper with a sports section" (Reader Reaction 1981a). Another collector, from Farmville, Virginia, wrote in 1981 of how Stommen had used *SCD* to help him promote a book he had written. He said that the old *SCD* had reminded him of a "hometown newspaper" and wrote, "I must admit that I have mixed emotions regarding your company buying the publication. With the large operation you have, I hope that you can still keep a style of relationship with collectors that the Stommens did in the past. . . . I have never met John Stommen or any of his family, but after receiving *SCD* for 2½ years, it is somewhat similar to losing an old friend" (Reader Reaction 1981c). By 1986, *SCD* editor Lemke was responding in the paper to accusations of dealer greed and *SCD* detachment from collectors. Lemke (1986) wrote, "It may surprise you to know that when [the] hobby business is at its best, we get the most complaints."[4]

In many ways Lemke's quotation suggested an interesting dilemma. In responding to his readers' complaints, Lemke avoided confronting questions of why adult men were interested in baseball cards in the first place, and instead asked, in effect, If business is good, why isn't everybody happy? But for many adult collectors and hobbyists, their attachment and interest in baseball cards stemmed from a need to hold on to elusive encounters with the past. This is what they had invested in the hobby, and it was as valuable as money. To those who complained to *SCD,* good business also meant that their hobby was being taken away from them. The conflicting emotions expressed by hobbyists illustrate that there is generally more to baseball card collecting than naked greed and that corporations do not have total control over the hobby's meanings. Chapters 2 and 3 look at the hobby from a grassroots perspective to understand what adult collectors have invested in their baseball cards and in their collecting practices.

2

Venues of Exchange and Adult Collecting

The adult baseball card collecting hobby in the Upper Midwest was booming during the time period in which I observed it. This boom provided a unique opportunity to examine how audiences participated in the use of "mass culture" commodities to produce a relatively grassroots form of popular culture. Perhaps the most public arenas I observed for such expression within the local baseball card collecting hobby were the regular shows that took place each weekend. These attracted thousands of adults and children from across the Upper Midwest. Beneath the festive surface of these events, however, there were a number of subtle conflicts concerning the definition and meaning of baseball card collecting. Many were attracted to it out of a sense of belonging, but this also meant creating distinctions of who belonged and who did not, particularly as adult collecting grew increasingly pluralistic, its boundaries ever harder to define.

Shows were at the center of this tension. They were public events that demonstrated a collective enthusiasm over baseball cards, and they were the hub of social activity within the local hobby. However, they were not explicitly organized around any common appreciation of baseball cards, but were instead venues for exchange. One did not even need to be a sports fan to attend or participate. The nostalgic images circulated at baseball card shows tended to speak to the sensibilities of white, middle-class men, but this common appreciation of a commercial object created something quite short of a community.

The Social Organization of Baseball Card Shows

The baseball card shows I observed varied widely in size and dimension. Promoters of small shows would usually rent a motel conference room, sometimes with only space enough for fifteen or twenty card tables, whereas promoters of large shows would rent gymnasiums, hockey arenas, empty storefronts, or large conference rooms with space for sixty-five to ninety tables. Some shows charged no admission fee, whereas others charged between fifty cents and three dollars per person per day. Some promoters held regular biweekly shows, whereas others held one only once or twice a year. Some hired a dazzling array of former athletes as autograph guests, sometimes including two or more Hall of Famers at once. During the span of my research, local shows featured baseball legends such as Willie Mays, Mickey Mantle, Hank Aaron, Lou Brock, Willie McCovey, Harmon Killebrew, Warren Spahn, and Eddie Matthews. Other promoters never hired a single autograph guest. These differences were important. At times they seemed to mark whether a show was "inside" or "outside" the area's most important hobby activity. One would tend to see the same dealers behind tables at the larger shows. These people had an enormous volume of both new and old material to sell and had the biggest displays. At smaller shows, one tended to find smaller dealers, people who lacked large collections of older cards but were selling prepackaged sets of current cards.

Still, there were a number of general similarities among all of the shows I attended. Usually one entered after paying somebody sitting behind a card table at the entrance, which was not simply a ticket counter but also a display area for future show advertisements, raffles, or want ads. At a number of large shows where autograph guests appeared, promoters sold eight-by-ten-inch glossy photos of the players on tables next to the ticket counter. Inside the show, promoters usually arranged a set of tables around the rim of the room and one or more islands of tables in the middle. In doing so they simultaneously created corridors for those attending and limited access to the areas behind the tables, where dealers would set up. Those attending would walk in patterned queues, strolling slowly from table to table, looking down at displays of cards.

When I entered shows, I was almost always somewhat disoriented by the volume of displays. Although dealers would often keep boxes of merchandise behind them or under the tables, they usually made much of what they sold visible to customers. Most often they would place rare, vintage baseball cards on the table in glass cases. Sometimes these were neatly displayed, with cards in plastic pockets, price tags carefully placed on them. Other times, dealers would stack cards in these cases in a somewhat random manner. Some dealers would illuminate their cases with desk lamps, making their cards seem like rare pieces of art; others would place baseball cards in rows of binders usually cataloged by year or team. They sold boxes of unopened wax packs, from both current and past years, which were stacked on their tables. These boxes were usually very colorful and loud, designed as display cases to be used in drug and grocery stores.

Occasionally dealers would strategically post cards on vertical pieces of cardboard to attract attention. One dealer who was a graduate student in communications told me that he consciously did this to draw the eyes of browsing customers from the tabletops. Others had similar ideas and would tack handmade signs above their tables advertising products and services. They advertised not only cards but also a whole range of other souvenirs and memorabilia: "Official 'Rawlings' Baseballs Sold Here"; "Wanted to Trade—I Have Lots to Trade for Older Mint Cards!!! Let's Trade! (Pre-1970 Stars and Commons Needed)"; "Buy! Sell! Trade! *Paying Cash for Cards*"; "Koinz and Kardz: The Mad City Buying Machine, We Want to Buy Your Quality Koinz and Kardz." Some signs were hand painted or drawn, whereas others were professionally designed and printed. It was important for some dealers to advertise that they would buy cards or trade them with customers, for many dealers refused to do this, and customers often attended shows with cards from their own collections, hoping to make some deals. It was also important that dealers have a good spot for their displays. Some dealers, for instance, insisted on being placed against a wall so that customers could see their signs and advertisements more easily. Others needed space for metal shelves they used to stack cases of cards and to advertise prices. Dealers often used mass-produced posters or advertisements for their displays. One dealer placed a life-size cardboard cutout of pro football running back Hershel Walker in front of his table. It was not unusual to see posters of star athletes such as Michael Jordan, Kirby

Puckett, or Wayne Gretsky displayed in front of or behind tables. Dealers often recycled discarded items from commercial culture to exhibit their cards. One man, for instance, used an old Plexiglas Timex watch case, the kind one finds in drugstores. In addition, dealers sold a variety of merchandise other than baseball cards. These items constituted a vivid form of display. Some vendors hung colorful sports-related T-shirts above or behind their tables. Others sold nostalgic watercolor paintings of former and current baseball players, or prints of photo-realist paintings of old baseball parks. Walking the aisles of a baseball card show meant confronting a panoply of merchandise: baseballs, bats, posters, autographed photos, trophies, old major-league uniforms, equipment actually used by players, pins, hats, Wheaties boxes, souvenir cans and bottles, frames, old programs and ticket stubs, baseball "action figures," and binders and plastic sheets for storing and cataloging cards. It appeared that collectors did not deem any item connected to baseball too trivial to be merchandised. Some sold paychecks that had been endorsed by famous baseball players, and one baseball card shop owner I met even sold a rag Tony Perez used to wipe the sweat from his forehead (the shop owner was careful to show me that one could still make out the stains on the towel).

The display of merchandise was not limited to tables or posters. Customers exhibited a display of what they consumed simply in what they wore to shows. Those who attended dressed in remarkably similar ways, wearing baseball caps with professional or college team logos, windbreakers with the name of a local softball team on the back, pro-team jackets, football and baseball jerseys, sports team T-shirts, and other items of wearable memorabilia. Others would wear variations of such clothing to express something particular about themselves. One married couple whom I often saw at shows would each wear black POW-MIA T-shirts and baseball caps, along with camouflaged army fatigue pants, to each event they attended.

The most important activity for one to learn at a show was how to bargain. The language of card shows centered on trading, and collectors often participated in exchanges with a great deal of seriousness. When I stood behind a table helping a dealer during one show in 1990, I was surprised by the level of animosity I felt from customers who wanted to make deals. Collectors would approach me and demand answers to questions: "What number is that card?"

31

"What's the Greenwell rookie worth?" "Do you have any '83 Donruss sets?" I was not always able to provide immediate answers to these questions, and this often made collectors impatient or angry.

One customer in particular became quite upset when I charged him sales tax for a 1988 Topps set that he was buying. He alleged that dealers never really paid sales tax, but rather added it onto the listed price of a card and then pocketed the extra money. Although show promoters almost always required dealers who set up tables to have a state sales tax number, baseball card dealers were often independent business operators who dealt in cash and could get away with a certain amount of cheating if they so desired. This particular customer became both angry and distrustful when he was charged a sales tax, and he demanded a receipt. The dealer I was working for wrote out a receipt, but this did not satisfy the customer, who said he wanted a "real" receipt. The dealer then told the customer to come to his store and get one from the cash register.

In fact, this particular dealer kept careful records of the cards and inventory he sold, and did not cheat on his taxes. However, he too took a remarkably serious approach to trading and bargaining at shows. When I arrived, for instance, he complained that the first four people who approached his table asked if he would buy their cards. He told me that he did not pay $130 per table to *buy* baseball cards.

On a superficial level, the kinds of behavior I observed at shows did not seem like very much fun. For leisure-time activities, baseball card shows appeared to involve a significant level of distrust, anxiety, and outright hostility. Rather than being arenas for a mutual and playful appreciation of baseball card collecting, they more often resembled the hard-nosed competition of a commodity exchange. In fact, one of the greatest ironies I observed was that collectors and dealers often reported being most annoyed at shows when dealing with children, even though the adult hobby sprang primarily from the idealized popular memories of childhood play.

Children comprised a significant proportion of those attending shows. In a line outside a suburban show in August 1989, I counted fifteen preadolescent boys, two preadolescent girls, fifteen teenage males, no teenage females, twenty-eight adult men, and five adult women. A significant number of dealers at shows were teenage boys, and fathers would often take their younger children (usually boys) to these events. Promoters frequently allowed children into shows for free, or would at least offer a discount to kids twelve or younger, and would sell refreshments such as hot dogs and soda to keep families at a show longer. Some dealers would allow their sons and daughters to help out behind the table.

Nevertheless, youths were often treated as intruders who acted out of line simply by participating at a show. Adult men regularly became somewhat annoyed by what they saw as children's obnoxious behavior. At one show a young boy walked up to a table and said, "Sir, can I return a card?" The dealer asked, "Is there a reason why?" The boy hesitated and then said, "I'll take half price." The man agreed to this but frowned and shook his head as the boy walked away. Some collectors I interviewed felt that the kind of bargaining in which this boy engaged was symbolic of a lost innocence, and others simply found it annoying. A twenty-six-year-old engineer who dealt nearly every weekend framed the behavior of children at baseball card shows as a metaphor for what he saw as society's deteriorating standards and traditional values:

Everything's so different nowadays than when we were kids. Kids are just so spoiled. I don't know, I have little nieces in town. They're just so spoiled. They go to the show and they just have their parents whipping out bills like you wouldn't believe. They buy stuff, they're a lot more smart about collecting. But they don't seem like they really have as much fun with it as I did when I was little.

Ironically, this man actively participated in turning baseball card collecting into an adult collector's pastime, as he was a dealer who made money selling baseball cards at shows. Other dealers I spoke with were a bit more self-conscious of their position in relation to preadolescent collectors and understood that they could not blame children for what had happened to the hobby they knew when they were young. During one interview, a forty-four-year-old utility company clerk and baseball card dealer named Kevin addressed children and greed at baseball card shows by discussing his function as a dealer in terms of paternal responsibility:

It's easy being older than them. It's easy to accept their abrasiveness or outspokenness as annoyance, interruption. That's part of the age difference. You find that all out when you're a parent. There are times when you don't want that little rug rat bugging you. But you have the responsibility to the child.

Well, as an entrepreneur, on the other side of that table, the fact that you set up your wares, your product on that table, you really should try your best to be decent to the person on the other side. Because after all, they are the ones that are more or less making it worth your while to be there. . . . I do get tired of the child stopping at the table, has a box, a binder of cards. But how else are you going to get started? I mean, you can see their enthusiasm. They're enjoying what they're doing. They get caught up in it. The emotions are running wild, and for the few youngsters that aren't emotional that seem to be quite reserved, you know that their stomachs are kind of churning because their eyes are getting kind of big, because they can see all this and they have to make decisions. It takes a lot of gumption for some of these youngsters, I think, just to speak up and ask an old fart like myself, "Are you buying?" or, "Would you like to look at my cards? Would you trade?" And I think that's where the idea of being an adult, father figure, whatever you want to call it, [is important]. You have to be patient with the younger people.

Kevin eloquently and sympathetically described the tension between men and boys at shows. However, his admonition to adults to be "patient" with children cuts against the grain of the predominant structure of shows in many ways. His discussion indicates that shows were not only about men nostalgically returning to their boyhood hobbies, but also about teaching boys to be men in a world of tough male competition.

I witnessed numerous times the tension between boys and men evident not only in trading practices, but also in the ways each group appreciated baseball. At one show, an adult man was trying to impress upon a boy who looked to be his son the importance of two players featured in a set of old photographs that were framed and autographed. "See, that's Roger Maris and that's Ty Cobb. That's what they looked like." The boy's eyes were slightly glazed over until he spotted another photo and yelled out, "There's Kirby Puckett!" The man was silent for a moment and then said in a somewhat irritated voice, "That's right." The boy reached for the Puckett photo, but the man moved the boy's hand away, saying, "Don't touch."

If boys were treated with little respect at shows, women were treated with even less, although they often were the ones primarily in charge of the children. At least some women were present at nearly every show, but they were rarely there as independent collectors or hobbyists. More often, they were the wives, sisters, partners, parents, or guardians of male collectors. I noticed that mothers often had the difficult task of keeping track of more than one child at a crowded show, or of explaining to their children basic economic principles about budgeting and spending. The women I met were marginalized at shows, and many had trouble maintaining interest. Discussing her reason for being behind the table at one show, a middle-aged woman who had traveled more than two hundred miles to the show told me of her husband's interest in baseball cards. Raising her eyebrows in a way that could have denoted either pride or sarcasm, she told me, "I don't think there's anybody here who knows statistics like my husband." When I asked whether she would be returning to a show the following week with her husband and son (who were behind the table with her but were completely ignoring her), she replied, "Next week I don't think I'm coming along. I don't think I'm essential."

At another show, a woman was earnestly trying to keep up with her teenage son. As he sped down the crowded aisles ahead of her, she tried to show interest in his activity. Passing one table, she asked him, "Did you see the Batman poster?" He dismissed this comment, saying, "Mom, you only show me stuff you think I'll like." His mother replied, "I just thought you would think it was neat." This boy's comment to his mother hints that any suggestion she made would have been tainted simply by her having thought of it.

At shows, a particularly male experience with sports spectatorship was made to seem valuable, special, and meaningful. Similarly, shows were primarily intended for and enjoyed by white people. Minorities were never explicitly barred from entering any show I attended (at large shows one could usually spot a few African American or Asian American faces), but shows idealized a brand of baseball nostalgia that seemed to speak particularly to white middle-class men.

One can see this in part by examining the class backgrounds of collectors I surveyed and interviewed. From my sample I found that the adult occupations of collectors at shows tended to span a relatively wide range, from unemployed blue-collar workers to white-collar professionals. Yet a surprising number of these men came from very similar class backgrounds, most often growing up within modest working-class or lower-middle-class families with fathers who were breadwinners and mothers who principally stayed at home.

This illustrates an important historical and demographic dimension to the hobby: adult collectors who attended shows were part of a large generation raised during an era when the Victorian model of the patriarchal nuclear family was reemerging (May 1988; Ehrenreich 1989). Despite their working-class occupations (and the fact that many remembered their mothers as having worked), the vast majority reported that their fathers were the family breadwinners, and mothers were "housewives," "stayed at home," or were "domestic engineers." Collectors' parents were able to get by mostly on one wage and still have discretionary income for their children to engage in the world as consumers.

Such prosperity, however, did not bless all of working-class America during the 1940s, 1950s, and 1960s. In particular, minority groups migrating to urban areas for work experienced deprivation and housing shortages as a result of discrimination and segregation, unequal pay, lack of seniority on the job, overcrowded neighborhoods, and police harassment (Lipsitz 1988). What is more, the suburbs that whites occupied were often restricted ones that covertly discriminated through practices such as redlining and blockbusting. It is significant that the only African American in my interview sample grew up not in a "traditional" nuclear family, but rather in one in which both his mother and father had to work full-time outside the home. Because baseball cards were something collectors nostalgically recalled from their childhoods, the racial composition of the collecting hobby suggests that perhaps the adults I observed were expressing aspects of experiences that were in large part defined by race as well as gender.

Evidence for racial division is further borne out in the prices of cards at shows. Nationwide, cards from the 1950s that featured white players tended to sell for higher prices than comparable ones of African American or Latino players.[1] The most dramatic example is the comparison of the 1952 Topps card featuring Mickey Mantle, which has sold for more than $25,000 at baseball card auctions, and the card featuring Willie Mays from the same Topps set, which never received even half that amount. This despite the fact that throughout both men's careers Mays outperformed Mantle in home runs, hitting, baserunning, and defense. In addition, the history of major-league baseball's own racism and segregation was often completely absent from shows. Negro League players were rarely acknowledged in photos or memorabilia of pre–World War II baseball, and some of the game's most notable bigots, such as Adrian Anson and Ty Cobb, were featured on some of the most valued items of memorabilia.

Yet shows also evidenced conflict concerning this primarily white audience's relationship to race. Dealers often displayed prominent images of famous African-American and Latino players, particularly contemporary stars such as Kirby Puckett, Cecil Fielder, Barry Bonds, Dave Winfield, José Canseco, and Roberto Alomar. In addition, fans lined up by the hundreds and paid more than ten dollars apiece for autographs by African American Hall of Famers such as Lou Brock and Willie McCovey. Despite the racial composition of the collecting public and its nostalgic appreciation of baseball, hobbyists celebrated the African American and Latino players whose playing styles and cultural backgrounds changed the game.

In addition, even though the baseball card collecting public I observed was relatively homogeneous, the exchange practices that characterized shows tended to undermine any real social cohesion among collectors. During the course of my research, I tried to find out whether there was a group that appreciated cards together in any sort of way, an organization or club made up of baseball card collectors. There was, in fact, one such group in the area, called the Midwest Collectors' Club, or MCC. What I discovered about this group and its history told me a great deal about the baseball card collecting hobby, its relationship to issues of race and gender, and the tensions that I observed so frequently at shows.

The MCC

I began to learn about the MCC during my earliest interviews with collectors. The informants I spoke with vaguely knew about the group, and some were even members, but few were actively involved or cared much about it. After a number of interviews, I finally found an active member named Bob, a forty-year-old pharmacist. He explained to me that although membership in the club had increased in recent years, most of those who joined it were only peripherally involved. In large part he blamed this on the hobby's local and national growth during the 1980s:

At one time, the club was the only one promoting shows, but now there are so many different promoters that the functioning of the club may be coming to an end. . . . What we've really tried to do [is] to get out and do things. You know, go to [baseball] games and that, and [all we've had is] just total apathy. . . . Everybody else just blows it off.

To illustrate his point, Bob told me that the MCC had bought forty tickets to an upcoming pro basketball game. Even though club membership had grown to more than three hundred people, he had only managed to sell ten tickets. At one time, when the hobby had been small in the area, the club had, in fact, assumed a more prominent role for local collectors. It promoted small monthly "meetings" (which were really small shows) held each week at a suburban mall, and it sponsored one or two large, nationally advertised shows every year. These had been, as Bob said, among the only large shows promoted in the area: "There was like about three big shows a year and then the monthly meetings. That was all. And there wasn't a lot going on. You always saw the same people."

The club began in the mid-1970s as a small-scale organization of men who as individuals had enjoyed collecting baseball cards but had not known that others in the area might be involved in the hobby as well. These men contacted one another through a register of baseball card enthusiasts that a hobbyist published and distributed nationally. They first met at a restaurant to plan the club and soon would meet with each other regularly, rotating from the basement of one member's house to another's garage. At this early point in its history, the organization was rather informal and private. Still, its members wanted it to grow, so they printed a small newsletter, which attracted more people. Soon the organization was too big for its membership to meet in house basements, so they moved to the lower-level meeting rooms of the mall where they sponsored their monthly meetings. By the late 1970s the mall management allowed the MCC to move its meetings, free of charge, into the main public plaza. In addition, the shopping center advertised the club meetings on its parking-lot marquee. By the beginning of the 1980s, the MCC had become the center of a rapidly growing hobby. Many collectors interviewed who had been part of the MCC in its early years remembered it positively. Steve, a baseball card shop owner and Kmart employee in his mid-forties, portrayed the organization as more genuine and sincere than the contemporary hobby, particularly in its rules of exchange:

> What I think was the best thing about the club: we would always swap. Now, you know, if you try to deal with anybody, they want to talk dollars, how much is it worth to you. I think the thing you're giving me is worth more or less, you know. But we used to, if I had something that somebody wanted or vice versa, I couldn't believe the help I got. A lot of camaraderie there.... It's just a good group. We kind of helped one another.

As discussed earlier, exchange has been a central component of baseball card collecting since it originated. Bob's complaints indicate that the club ceased to function outside of the exchange practices it promoted. For Steve, however, the MCC had allowed for a kind of friendly bartering among comrades. He portrayed members as mutually valuing certain cards, not because they were listed next to a favorable figure in a price guide, but because they brought the owner some intrinsic level of pleasure and satisfaction. Because members understood one another, according to Steve, they were able to create a hobby that was cooperative and mutually affirming.

Yet by the mid-1980s there were signs that the MCC might not be able to control the direction of the hobby. Baseball card collecting had become so popular nationally that card prices had inflated to record levels. In 1985, in a development symptomatic of these changes, a popular local newspaper and magazine store chain began to sell vintage baseball cards. The concerns and conflicts that developed because of such growth disrupted the MCC in a controversy involving the club's new president, a lawyer named Dave, who not only brought a new vision of what the organization should be, but was also the club's only African American member.

I first learned of Dave when I was interviewing Bob about the MCC. Bob told me of a past president who had attempted to take over the organization and to steal money from its members. When I asked about this person further, Bob warned me that I should be careful. Dave, he said, was a powerful and vindictive lawyer who promoted one of the region's largest shows and would sue me if he did not like what I wrote.

Dave was actually quite willing to meet me for two interviews and was open and frank about his dealings with the club. As I eventually learned, Bob's bitter and perhaps paranoid characterization of the former MCC president was largely the product of a controversy that had erupted over Dave's leadership. In 1984 Dave was the MCC's vice president and was scheduled to assume the top role in 1985. Before becoming president, however, he wanted to put forth a proposal to the club's membership. He had been helping to promote the club's annual shows when he discovered that the MCC had never been legally incorporated as a nonprofit or for-profit organization. This left its officers individually responsible for damages and debts that resulted from shows. In addition, he found that club officers were doing almost all of the work required to promote a show while the membership reaped the fruits of the officers' labor.

In the October 1984 MCC newsletter, Dave proposed that the club incorporate and be headed by a five-person "management team" led by the president. He explained that such a move was necessary because of the current informal structure of the organization and the ways in which officers were legally vulnerable. He wrote, "This type of exposure is senseless and potentially devastating."

The club membership overwhelmingly approved the proposal to incorporate, with 86 percent voting in favor. Over the next two years, the club grew to a record 417 members. The newsletter also expanded and improved, printing more articles introducing trivia quizzes, and using better graphics and a cleaner-looking typeface than the photocopied, typewritten print of previous newsletters. Nevertheless, Dave was often the target of complaints brought by a small but particularly prominent and long-standing set of members, including some founders of the MCC.

Probably the most vocal of Dave's critics was Max, a long-standing member who also promoted an annual show for his own profit. At the time, Max's show was the only large one in the region other than the club's, and most members did not object to his promoting it. Max, however, objected to a proposal by Dave to have the club promote an extra show annually. Too many shows, Max argued, would ruin the hobby. Of course, they would also provide increased competition for Max's own show. The self-serving nature of his complaints notwithstanding, Max was able to build support within the organization to challenge Dave's leadership.

In the early months of 1986, these tensions broke open into an argument about the structure of the club. Dave and several of his officers contended that they were fed up with the complaints and lack of help they received from club members like Max. As officers of an incorporated organization, they also requested financial compensation for their work. Simultaneously, Max organized a group within the MCC, made up of many longtime members, to protest the fact that Dave had not continued a club tradition of annually publishing the organization's financial status. The request for this information was also a thinly veiled accusation that the club's officers, especially Dave, had been lining their pockets with MCC funds, particularly those supposedly received from a large, successful show in 1985.

Dave proposed a referendum on the continuation of the club's new management structure and the formation of a separate, for-profit promotional outfit to run shows and to subsidize the club. Once again Dave won, gaining 70 percent of the vote. Still, his critics did not give up and were able to persuade those who attended a meeting that August to hold yet another referendum. Under the stress of this situation, Dave and the club's other officers decided to resign. In the summer edition of the newsletter, Dave and three members of the management team concluded their letter of resignation with the declaration, "we will . . . maintain a VERY visible presence on the [local] hobby scene."

Terry, a fifty-year-old computer company employee and one of the founders of the club, recalled that he had been critical of Dave's leadership. In fact, he had signed the letter that had called for financial disclosure by club officials. He characterized the crisis as a "rough period" for the MCC and placed the blame squarely on Dave's shoulders:

> We had this president [who] would see that if he could incorporate the club somehow, he could make money for himself. Up until this time, it had been a private, or it'd been a nonprofit deal. . . . None of us ever got compensated at all. Not even a minimal hundred dollars a year or something like that. Nothing. . . . He, in effect, took over the club.

Terry not only found Dave's request for compensation distasteful, he practically accused Dave of single-handedly infusing the local hobby with greed. Like Steve, he presented the club in its early years as free from monetary corruption, a genuine and honest hobby made up of collectors who truly appreciated their cards. "I don't even think there was anybody in it to supplement their income," he told me. Nevertheless, he contradicted himself during our interviews and had a hard time resolving his conflicting memories surrounding the hobby:

> From the very beginning, people wanted to make money. People could see that buying and trading was a way of helping their own collections. . . . Nobody was in the hobby at that time as a full-time business, or as a part-time business, but it was a way of increasing the value of their own collections.

Collectors were supposedly enjoying the pure hobby of baseball card collecting, but they were also concerned about the monetary value of their collections. Although no collectors were in the hobby to supplement their incomes, they always wanted to make money. Such contradictions led Dave to conclude that his critics were guilty of "hypocrisy." This might have been true, but Terry indicated that perhaps money was symbolic of a bigger issue involved in their criticism of Dave. Terry felt that Dave, "in effect, took over the club." Dave acknowledged that he represented a kind of threat to many in the organization's membership:

> I think the big problem was that I had pretty big plans and I went through with them. I was smarter than most of the people in the hobby, definitely smarter than most of the dealers, and I had the vision to see some of the business opportunities there. . . . I pointed out to the guys I was working with that there was the potential there to make a lot of money, compared to what we were doing before. . . . We were a little arrogant too, I admit that. But I'd say there was a lot of resentment.

The resentment had a great deal to do with the ambitions that Dave articulated as well as with the changes that began to take place within the hobby during the 1980s. But it also had something to do with the fact that Dave was an African American. Dave himself felt this, and although most other collectors whom I interviewed about the incident denied or downplayed the significance of racism, they also hinted that race was not an insignificant part of the controversy. Doug, a thirty-nine-year-old baseball card shop owner who had been an ally of Dave's within the organization, brought up the issue of race before I did during one of our interviews. When I asked him about the MCC controversy, he responded, "Yeah, I don't know if that was partially racist or what, but they didn't like one of the officers." Larry, a full-time dealer in his early thirties, was a member of Dave's management team. Although he only grudgingly accepted that race was a factor in Dave's problems in the club, he acknowledged that it may have been important:

[Dave's] not somebody who goes around pointing the finger and crying racist. He's said it to me privately. I've heard, not anybody locally. I've heard other people say it. I've never heard anything overt. . . . but it's possible, because he would be viewed—well, I know him. He can be like that. He can be viewed by a lot of people that are looking for that type of thing as an arrogant black guy, see. And so maybe that was part of it.

Significantly, both Dave and Larry used the word "arrogant," Larry explicitly linking it with "black," to describe why Dave so passionately offended some club members. This seems to have made Dave an easy foil for the changes taking place in the local hobby and a target for the resentment stirred up among local hobbyists as their "community" was being fragmented by a consumer-driven market. In fact, Dave was not to blame for the apathy in the MCC during the late 1980s, for the emergence of individually promoted shows in the area, or for the appropriation of baseball card auctions by home shopping channels on cable television, all of which helped to make the club less and less important to hobbyists. What MCC members' anger toward Dave does suggest, however, is that he represented something bigger than himself: a threat to the "purity" of a hobby.

The competition that independently sponsored shows represented with regard to the hobby's boundaries erupted in another controversy a year later, this one highlighting issues of gender more than race. Not long after the MCC had resolved its conflict over Dave's leadership, a club member named Wes, a second-grade teacher in his early thirties, began to organize his own show separately from the club's. Wes got the idea after realizing how much money he was spending at Max's show:

I went to Max's show and he had Stan Musial there, and I walked in and I think I spent six dollars for an autograph. So I bought two autographs. I bought a ball, [spent] two dollars to get in, and [bought] an eight-by-ten. That was, like, twenty-six dollars, and I hadn't even been in to buy cards yet. And I thought, this is incredible. And I looked behind me, and I looked at the line going outside the door, and I thought, if you take even ten dollars per person, there's five or six hundred people out there.

Wes did not anticipate that promoting another show would cause much friction among the club's members. Yet he was, in his words, the first "outsider" to dare to promote a show. Even Dave, who went on to promote his own annual show after leaving the MCC, was respected enough to be considered a "legitimate" promoter. But as a newcomer to the club, Wes drew fire from its members:

> They were doing a lot of real bad press on me in their little newsletter that they put out, saying that I wasn't a member of the club. What business did I have coming in and doing the shows? And I was strictly in it for profit and all that, which I was. And I mean, I didn't hide that at all. I said, yeah, I am.

Wes further infuriated members by scheduling his show only a week before one promoted by a long-standing MCC member named Mike, whose show was a benefit in memory of his late daughter. Wes claimed that he could get the auditorium only on that weekend. After hiring his autograph guests and sending in his deposit, Wes let Mike know about his plans:

> He said, "well, cancel [the guests] and change." He said, "I'm going to bury you," and [was] very threatening. And I said, "I guess I can't do anything from this point. I guess we're just going to have to do our best and good luck to both of us." [I felt] a little anger at the time, but he was still threatening. But on the other side, maybe a little guilt on mine because I was the one cutting him by a week. And then his didn't go well and mine was a huge success.

This despite the fact that the MCC called for a boycott of Wes's show in its newsletter. The boycott call initially scared Wes, but he eventually realized that he had "really over-estimated" members' power. Most dealers and collectors cared more about the show's autograph guests, who had been former heroes for the local major-league baseball team, and the location of the show, just off a major interstate highway exit in a well-traveled suburb, than they did about the MCC. By this time, according to Wes, the club's membership had dropped to only about two hundred, although the hobby was rapidly expanding in the region.

The resentment that Wes stirred up concerning the local control of the hobby flared again the following year when Wes signed a female wrestler as an autograph guest. He had been having trouble finding a baseball player who would be available for his show when a booking agent suggested the wrestler, who offered to sign posters of herself, charging fans five dollars apiece. Wes created an advertisement including a reprint of the poster that the wrestler would be signing, in which she posed in a bikini. The editor of the MCC newsletter, however, refused to run the ad, claiming it was "pornographic." Furthermore, he alleged in the next newsletter that Wes had hired somebody for his show who had posed for *Playboy* magazine, and he attacked Wes for corrupting the hobby: "They were real upset that . . . that I had a woman coming in. It's not for kids, it's for adults. . . . So right away they were saying, kind of accusing me of putting on a pornographic show."

Like Dave, Wes had presented the club with a challenge to its centrality within the local hobby, and once again club members had responded by expressing resentment. Because Wes had signed a female autograph guest, and particularly one who exhibited her sexuality in a flamboyant way, the club could easily represent Wes as polluting the purity of the hobby or introducing into their fantasy of boyhood innocence an image that was "not for kids."

This is not to deny that Wes was indeed using an objectified and eroticized image of female sexuality to sell tickets to his show. But this event also illustrates the importance of gender to the hobby. The argument against the female wrestler that Wes reported was not that she represented something harmful to women, but rather that her presence corrupted the hobby "for kids."

As much as the MCC served as a conservative institution with regard to the hobby's boundaries, neither Dave nor Wes really challenged the legitimacy of such boundaries. They both reported drawing their primary satisfaction not from making money but from the feelings of importance and accomplishment they gained through promoting. Dave told me, "The primary motivation for me now is that I have the reputation for putting on probably the best shows in [the city]." Likewise, Wes had become more motivated by the challenge that the MCC gave him than he had by the financial rewards of promoting. When Mike issued his threat, Wes remembered thinking, "I'm going to show him that I can hold my own. And now it's a little competitive feeling, I guess, when I see the other shows going on. It's who is doing the best show."

For both Dave and Wes, baseball card shows assumed a meaning bigger than the hobby itself. Promoting a show certainly meant being important within the hobby scene, but just as significantly, the hobby provided a context for these adults to express their identities and sense of self-worth. Although both Dave and Wes were critical of the local network of collectors, the hobby was something they both cared about.

When Terry first set out to organize the MCC in the 1970s, he sought to make his private hobby more public and to create a community of collectors with a genuine, common bond to baseball cards. For him and for others who resented the changes that Dave brought about within the MCC, this community was, by definition, an exclusive one in which everybody knew and understood one another. The expansion of adult baseball card collecting meant not only an infusion of money and greed but also a disruption of boundaries as the club and its most central members became a less important and less vital aspect of the local hobby.

In large part, the fragmentation of the baseball card collecting public during the 1980s was the result of a hobby in which exchange was the central activity. Because of this, loyalties to fellow collectors ran thin when pitted against the promise of bigger shows with more dealers, more cards, and better autograph guests. But this focus on exchange could not be blamed only on greedy dealers or even on the aggressive marketing strategies of baseball card companies. It was imbedded in the very practices of collecting, even among the most traditional of collectors. The next chapter focuses on hobbyists and their collecting practices, exploring the significance of exchange and its relationship to the emotions that collectors invested in their hobby.

3

Collecting Sets

During the period of my research, adult collectors in the Upper Midwest experienced their hobby both publicly and privately. It would be a profound understatement to say that no two collectors engaged with their cards in exactly the same way, yet there were noteworthy commonalities and trends in collecting behavior. One of the most important was the phenomenon of collecting sets. Most collectors used the term *set* to refer to all of the cards produced by a company during a particular year. Collectors also sometimes created their own sets, defining a particular category and attempting to complete it. The collection of sets was the most common collecting practice within my interview sample. Nineteen out of the thirty men I interviewed, for example, reported that they either had collected or were collecting full company sets. Of the remaining eleven men, five collected more self-defined sets, such as "oddball" cards, rookie cards, and teams.[1]

The collection of sets is noteworthy for two major reasons. First, it illustrates an active way in which a popular culture audience involves itself with a form of commercial entertainment. At the very least, the act of collecting a set of either new or old cards requires some level of organization, active effort, knowledge, and, at times, dogged tenacity. Second, and more important, hobbyists who pieced together sets provided me with insights into baseball card collecting as a particularly male sports fan subculture. The pleasures and fantasies that made sets meaningful to the collectors I interviewed had an important relationship to gender. The processes involved in recapturing a set of baseball cards were evocative of the rituals and play that the men interviewed remembered as surrounding baseball cards when they were boys. The act of collecting sets as adults brought them back into the kind of all-male relationships they recalled from their preadolescent years. In addition, the set collectors I observed attempted to create a coherent order with their cards, one that linked them to this idealized past without any contradictions, gaps, or digressions. By striving for such seamless connections, however, adult collectors separated their cards from many of the playful games and interactions that had made these objects meaningful to children during the 1950s, 1960s, and 1970s.

The separation of collected objects from the contexts in which they were originally meaningful, and their subsequent reification as constituents of a collected set, is not unique to baseball card collectors (see Stewart 1984; Danet and Katriel 1989). Yet baseball card collecting is also a fan subculture, and the importance of set collecting within it reveals a great deal about the men I observed and about their gendered orientation toward sports spectatorship. Henry Jenkins, in his work on female-based media fan cultures, borrows from the literary criticism of Michel de Certeau, who coined the term *textual poachers* for readers who appropriate aspects of literary texts for their own purposes. Jenkins sees fans, like textual poachers, as cultural nomads operating "from a position of marginality and social weakness" in relation to the cultural forms they enjoy. They have very little creative control over the production of commercial culture around them, but they can negotiate their way through it, actively "poaching" certain aspects of their media experiences and reassembling them in ways meaningful to their social experiences (1992, 26–27).

Jenkins draws two conclusions about fans as poachers and nomads. First, fans are social: their practices gain meaning from and are reinforced through interactions with others. Second, fans blur the boundaries between cultural producers and cultural readers: they create and circulate their own artistic formulations from the representations produced for them on television or within other forms of media culture.

These conclusions are both characteristic of the baseball card collectors I observed. Collectors published their own newsletters and magazines, promoted their own shows, and created their own displays for cards. Some even created and circulated their own baseball card sets. "Broders," cards illegally produced by legendary renegade sports fan George Broder, were widely distributed at shows. Such cards featured color photos of athletes printed on one side of a blank card, and were published without the licensing agreements necessary for the sale of such products. They illustrate fans' attempt to take control of media images by evading copyright laws meant to protect the interests of cultural producers above those of cultural consumers (Gaines 1991; Jenkins 1992, 25).

Yet the sports fan culture I observed differed in important, largely gendered, ways from the media fan culture that Jenkins describes. Jenkins argues that the female character of the fan groups he studied was important because those groups felt especially marginalized by the processes of media production, which, particularly in the case of science fiction, favored male audiences. Such fan cultures are especially nomadic, as they lack any close "proximity to writers and editors" who produce the texts from which they poach (48).

In contrast, baseball card and memorabilia collectors have a great many allies in the popular media. Entire sections of the newspaper are devoted to the interests of collectors' fan cultures, and the writers of those sections, often current or former collectors themselves, frequently recollect bittersweet memories of flipping cards and opening their first packs. This creates a remarkable bond of gender identity among some quite diverse groups of men. At the same time, it does not create the sense of marginality from mass-media production that many other fan cultures feel. The men I interviewed could often identify major newspaper writers such as Thomas Boswell or George Will who felt just the way they did about baseball.

This is not to say that collectors, like other fan cultures, were not trying to make sense of their own social experiences. But the texts they chose for this purpose, and the ways in which they put those texts together, did not often represent an attempt to create new alternatives. Rather, collecting reflected an effort to find and reestablish a stable sense of order from the cultural symbols of the collectors' past.

"Building" Sets

I observed two basic types of sets that collectors would strive for. Some collectors would work at obtaining sets of older cards. Men were often prompted to do so after they or their mothers found

49

(rather than threw away, as popular collecting folklore claimed) their old childhood collections. Such collections were usually incomplete sets, so collectors often sought to "fill them in," or buy the cards that were missing from their childhood collection. Because a set might include anywhere from three hundred to more than seven hundred cards, completing a set could be extremely time-consuming. Collectors could spend hundreds or even thousands of dollars, depending on the year of the cards they were looking for. The price of a card depended on a number of factors: its scarcity, its desirability (was the player a star, or was he a "common"?), and its condition. Collectors often used nationally published price guides to help them compare costs, and often adopted the standards of those guides. Because price guides placed in the highest-priced category cards in "mint" condition, most collectors sought the most pristine cards they could afford so that their collections would have "value." They usually avoided cards with bent corners, creases, off-center printing, or writing on them. Once they finished filling in a set, collectors often moved on to another, trying to fill in the gap of missing cards between their childhoods and the present.

The second kind of sets that collectors would buy were those of new cards. At any baseball card show or shop, collectors could purchase an already sorted full set of new cards produced by any of the five companies making baseball cards by 1990. These were called "factory sets," and often collectors would routinely buy all the factory sets produced by each company every baseball season.[2] With the proliferation of card sets by the early 1990s, however, many collectors found this to be a difficult task to manage financially and could not afford to keep up with all of the cards being produced. To acquire new sets, or even to afford older cards for sets they might have been trying to fill in, collectors often bought cases of new cards at wholesale prices. They would then open up the packs of cards in the cases and sort them into sets themselves. By doing so, they could get four or even five sets from a case, saving money on the cost per set. They could also potentially get a large number of duplicate cards that featured a valued contemporary star such as Cecil Fielder or Kirby Puckett. Collectors used such cards and sets to barter for other cards, either new or old, that they felt they needed.

Collectors often felt very proud of their sets and were somewhat protective of them. Despite the fact that they might be able to sell their sets for hundreds, perhaps even thousands, of dollars, many collectors I interviewed were like Tim, a junior marketing executive in his late twenties, who said he would never sell his set, even though it included some very valuable cards:

> Like I say, it's just a hobby for me. It's just the collecting; I like to — my goal is just to keep building my collection until I get a real nice collection. I feel if I ever have kids of my own and they want to start, then — I can give them some of mine, or we could do it together, or whatever.

Tim's orientation toward his set was not atypical. Many collectors not only valued their sets but saw the sets as extensions of themselves. Even dealers who no longer collected sets would speak of "crossing the bridge" from collecting to dealing, severing an important emotional tie to cards in the moment they decided to sell their sets. For Tim, who still owned many of the cards he had collected as a boy, his sets connected him not only to the past but also to the future: his potential children. What is perhaps most important here is that the past is remembered and the future is imagined through the baseball card set, which remains a stable, constant entity over time. It was part of Tim's childhood and, he hoped, might be part of his own child's as well.

Sets became important to collectors largely through the process of collecting them. This process was at least as important and as meaningful to many collectors as were the cards themselves. Barry, a thirty-one-year-old UPS delivery driver, characterized his collecting as "almost like an addiction." As with Tim, Barry's hobby centered on the collection of sets:

> I'm more of a set collector. I try to get the whole set. And yeah, that always makes you feel good when you complete a set. That's what you strive for. And it's really hard to do, especially in a lot of the older sets because of the financial . . . the prices of the cards are so high now. Those are the goals I do set, to complete the set. I know other people, that's what makes the hobby real good too.

Barry referred to his collecting practices as involving the "building" of sets, a common way of discussing the hobby. It conveyed the idea that a set was something one created through work, craftsmanship, and patience. Bob, the pharmacist mentioned in chapter 2, also used this language to describe his hobby. He told me during one of our interviews, "I'm a set builder." The process of building a set was so central to his collecting that he began to lose interest in baseball cards once he had succeeded: "I'm a goal-oriented person. I like to set goals and if you keep reaching them it takes the challenge away. And that's the way it was with the cards. Maybe I didn't set my goals high enough, like a million dollars or something."

The "goal-oriented" perspective that Bob discussed was a very important aspect of the individualistic and competitive orientation of set collecting. Many collectors worked out elaborate forms of trading, selling, and bartering cards to buy the ones they needed. They studied price guides, searched through card shops, attended shows, read publications, and even frequented garage sales and flea markets. They described their purchase of cards as a personal quest. Sometimes this alienated collectors from one another, causing them to act in selfish and petty ways. At the very least it made collecting, at its roots, a solitary activity, something one did ultimately for oneself.

The whole process of collecting sets in this manner was something collectors often reported as typical of their collecting practices as children. In fact, a sort of obsession with set collecting among kids was parodied by *Sports Illustrated* as far back as its first issue in 1954. This issue included a feature on baseball cards in which two columns bracketed a color centerfold illustrating the cards. The first column, by Martin Kane, detailed the marketing and contract wars taking place between the baseball card producers that year, Topps and Bowman. The second article was by Jerome Weidman, a father of two baseball-card-collecting boys. Both articles discussed collecting in a humorous manner, portraying it as a typically incomprehensible youth fad. In their humor, however, they conveyed an uneasiness with the desires and emotions that baseball cards evoked in children.

Weidman's essay began as a discussion of his bewilderment at the way baseball cards, objects he would normally have identified as useless advertisements for a product such as bubble gum, had become consumer objects that his children desired. He wrote of how his children discarded the bubble gum from baseball card packs but treasured the baseball cards, and he expressed dismay over the ways gum companies would manipulate their young audiences:

[T]o make certain that boys will continue to purchase bubble gum as steadily as alcoholics purchase gin, no bubble gum manufacturer publishes pictures of *all* the members of a given team. This is because our young baseball-card collectors trade their duplicates with other collectors. Thus, much too soon for the bubble gum manufacturers, every boy would own a complete set of 448 cards and be eliminated as a customer.

Weidman's article culminated with a story of how, on a summer-long family vacation in England, his sons realized that they did not have a card for Brooklyn catcher Roy Campanella. Weidman wrote that he had to have a friend ship a case of baseball cards to England in the middle of the family's trip. He made the case last throughout the entire summer, giving his sons only one pack to open each day. The boys found six Roy Campanellas but told their father on the plane ride home that they were missing one other card. Weidman ended the article recalling his reaction to the boys' dilemma: "[It] was awful funny, Dad, but the one card they couldn't seem to get was a Solly Hemus, and what did I think of that? . . . It required quite a bit of self-control on Dad's part not to tell them."

Weidman's column is about not only baseball cards but also his inability to direct his children's desires as he became less important to them than their baseball cards. Even a trip to England could not compete with these cardboard objects. He told his story clearly with tongue in cheek, but his complaints about his children's insatiable appetite for a form of commercial entertainment parallel the concerns about television and the 1950s nuclear family that Lynn Spigel has profiled (Spigel 1990, 73–97). He portrays his boys as thoughtless, passive, programmed, and shamelessly manipulated.

This kind of obsessive set collecting was certainly promoted by baseball card companies, but childhood collecting was not always as passively programmed an activity as Weidman presents it. Collectors often discussed trading with friends, bargaining over cards in the school yard or in their bedrooms, and trying to amass the best collection they could. Yet those interviewed also remembered the collecting of their childhoods as far more diverse than their adult hobby, which was so heavily oriented toward sets. When they recalled childhood collecting, they discussed a whole variety of games they would play with cards that, as adults, they had abandoned because such games were incompatible with set collecting. The adult hobby of the 1980s that I observed highlighted only the most competitive and manipulative aspects of childhood baseball card collecting.

In fact, some of the most successful adult collectors were those who had had the least playful collecting experiences as children. Thomas, an executive for a local candy distributor, remembered collecting his cards very privately, particularly after his family became the first to move to an isolated suburb when interstate highway construction leveled his inner-city neighborhood. His meticulous habits allowed him to preserve his cards in excellent condition, and he was very proud to point this out during our interview:

> From day one, I always . . . for some reason I was a neat freak. It was like I wanted my own cards. You know, my old . . . well, these are my old football cards from the sixties [showing them to me], and I mean you can see they're beautiful. The corners and . . . now, unfortunately, I don't have my baseball [cards]. I sold those about nine years ago. And, like everybody else did . . . but these are just, they're like new. I mean, it's unbelievable.

As an adult, Thomas was rewarded for the way he had collected as a child, establishing a small sports card side business from the profits he gained by selling his baseball card sets. However, he also noted that his childhood collecting habits meant he did not enjoy the kind of playful relations with other kids that so many associated with their collecting. Most notably, he did not engage in trading and would only buy cards new, because he wanted to keep them in the same condition as they were in the moment he bought them. Likewise, Larry, the full-time dealer referred to in chapter 2, recalled that he never engaged in fabled childhood games such as baseball card "flipping" when he was a boy. Instead, he remembered his collecting as very much a mirror of his adult collecting:

> I never did like card flipping. I never heard of that until I was an adult. . . . Not so much in school, but with friends from school, we did a lot of trading. I mean we were fanatics. Well, I mean like any kids, I guess. Into baseball and into baseball cards. I'd say back in '68, '69, '70, I had at least two real good friends who were constantly trying to make baseball card deals to add to our collections. You know, one kid had a card that you needed and you tried to get it from him.

Larry's recollections illustrate how set collecting, from a very early age, was linked to a competitive economic relationship with cards, one that mirrored the adult world of capital acquisition. Although Larry created friendships through the competitive trading and negotiating for cards that he described, these friends were at the same time potential stooges. Doug, the baseball card shop owner introduced in chapter 2, collected sets meticulously when he was a child. Like Larry, Doug built his collection by trading with friends. His memories emphasize, more than competition, the prominence of order that kept him from sharing his most treasured cards:

> I always traded with my friends. I had a rule that I would never trade if I only had one card. That was part of my collection, and that got stuck away. I would just pull out all the extra cards that I had. . . . [Other kids] thought that was my collection. But that would be just trading. I had as many probably, duplicates, as a lot of other kids would have in their collections. . . . My mother bought an Ethan Allen dresser drawers, a ten-drawer dresser, and I put my collection in there. . . . I organized it by teams. Anytime a player got traded, I'd put him from one box — pull him out of there — put him with the other ones.

John, a dealer and salesman in his late twenties, had similar memories of his private collection. Like Doug, John never traded any cards from his core collection: "I never traded anything other than duplicates." Unlike other kids, he was very concerned with keeping his cards orderly and in good condition. He conveyed this in a story he told about trading with his school friends:

> We did a lot of trading after school. We couldn't wait to get home. Didn't bring a lot of cards to school. There was this one kid. He had a paper route. I think he probably ripped off half of them [the cards], in the stores. But he was on a paper route and he had money coming in so he could spend his money the way he wanted to because he was the main paperboy in town. Well, he would bring them to school and show them and have them in his pocket the rest of the day, and go out and play kickball, or whatever, out in the yard and come back in. [The cards] would be all bent up and then [he would] want to trade them. And I'd say no. No dice.

In addition to engaging in discriminating trading practices, John would use his baseball cards to play an elaborate baseball board game.

He often played against his brother or his friends, but they did not always have the time to participate. As a result, he would play games against himself, using his cards to construct teams and leagues that would play entire seasons and championships. Although all of these collecting habits and games seem to foretell an individualistic adult hobby centered on set collecting, John also recalled a sense of excitement and camaraderie that he shared with his boyhood friends about collecting cards:

> After school you couldn't wait just to get home and go through the cards. Or run uptown and buy some. I can remember when . . . the worst feeling in the world is when the small . . . there was like two stores in that town. A very small town. And when they ran out of cards, it was like for the next week or so, what are you going to do? But as soon as they got the cards in, we were lined up outside.

John's recollections demonstrate that many collectors remembered their cards not only as things they had collected but also as a part of a world they had shared with their friends during their preadolescent years. Although they might have competed with one another over the cards, they also remembered seeking each other's friendship and using cards as an expression of common interests. Most adult collectors did not recall collecting sets meticulously when they were kids. Many traded cards, invented games with them, made drawings on them, and used them quite informally. Wes, the second-grade teacher whose show created a controversy with the MCC, recalled collecting only the biggest-named stars when he was a boy. He also remembered playfully using his cards in noncompetitive ways: "We would get together and trade. That would be about the only extent of games. And it was always to take the real unknown players, put them in your spokes with a clothespin, and just make the sound as your bike tires were going around."

A number of other collectors also remembered placing baseball cards in bicycle spokes for noise, an act that showed no regard for the condition of one's cards. It was also a form of play not organized around rule-bound competition as was trading. Adults also remembered sorting their cards into "all-star" teams and using statistics on the back of the cards to play one team against another.

Differences between childhood and adult collecting practices often were most apparent when collectors would discuss how they "ruined" their cards when they were young because of their disregard for the cards' "condition." Tim had one such memory:

> We didn't take real good care of them. I don't remember writing on cards too much. But I remember cutting them out one time. Just cutting the body outline so you didn't have any of the edges. We could have had a whole set, like the mid-sixties that my uncle gave us. We were just so stupid. What do six- or seven-year-olds know, you know?

Tim's reflection upon his own childhood play with cards as being "stupid" illustrates an important aspect of the adult hobby and its focus on set building. Although for many, childhood collecting often involved putting together sets or attending to condition, it also was more oriented toward playful, even noncompetitive activities. When a child drew a mustache on a player's face or placed a card in a bicycle spoke, he or she was using a card in an expressive and inventive way with others. However, the fetish regarding condition created a number of ironies within the adult hobby. For example, when Topps issued sets in series during the 1950s, 1960s, and early 1970s, each set included checklists so that kids could mark off which cards they had in their collections. Most kids used these checklists, thus ruining the cards' status as "mint" cards in the adult hobby. The most valuable checklists during the 1980s were those that had never been used and thus were of no value to their previous owners.

The kind of drawing on cards that Tim described illustrates how cards were being *used,* how they were a part of the way kids together would follow baseball as spectators. Even gambling games such as flipping, the piecing together of all-star teams, or trading, all of which were competitive activities, also involved kids in play with one another. The adult hobby, with its focus on completing sets of cards in mint condition, was a negation of such play. Rather, it placed the focus of collecting upon the individualistic acquisition and organization of cards.

All of this is not to say that the process of building a set was irrelevant. Set building for adults required going to shows, trading for cards, and interacting with others. Collectors reported that these processes in large part made their collections meaningful in ways that spoke to their gendered identities. To understand the gender dynamics involved in set building, it is important to examine the significance of the childhood collecting practices that collectors remembered.

Card Collecting, Sports Fandom, and Male Gender Identity

Modifying and updating the theories of sociologist Janet Lever (1976), Michael Messner has written of the centrality of competition and achievement to sports as a form of boys' play. Messner sees sports as socializing boys for their roles as men in a patriarchal culture by speaking to their already present ideas about gender roles and relations when they first begin to participate in team sports as seven- to nine-year-olds. Messner argues that gendered identity must be worked out by individuals as they go through the process of individuation, or the setting up of psychological boundaries between themselves and others around them. Within a patriarchal culture, boys most often work out this process by constructing boundaries along gendered lines, separating themselves particularly from their mothers. Messner notes that this is not only an individual, psychological process but also a social one. Social relations with others provide the context for the creation of such individual boundaries. Messner concludes that "the rule bound structure of sport" creates an important context in which boys are able to construct masculine identities. This is true not only for men who participate in sports but also for those who experience sports through mediated channels (such as television or baseball cards) as sports spectators (Messner 1990, 100–3; Chodorow 1978).

Such renderings of sports and gender socialization suggest a relatively clear-cut distinction between the play of boys and girls, as well as the relationship of such play to their maturation into men and women. This analysis may stem from the fact that Messner, by and large, draws his conclusions about children's sports from official, adult-monitored forms of play, such as Little League (Messner 1992, 24–41). But it also portrays child audiences as somewhat passively molded by the media forms and play activities that adults create for them. When I asked collectors about the memories they had of their hobby, they gave me a complex set of answers suggesting that they engaged in active forms of sports fandom as children and as adults. What's more, rather than preparing them for heterosexual masculinity, these forms of fandom often actually conflicted with their later heterosexual male identities.

Ironically, the less formal group relations of preadolescent sports, although largely all male, allowed more space for boys to accept girls as equals than did the heterosexual world of adolescence. Furthermore, most collectors recalled the carryover of preadolescent sports fan cultures into the teen world of heterosexual dating and pairing as being taboo or "uncool," boyish, and something they felt compelled to hide or abandon.

During interviews, collectors discussed their childhood hobby as a boy's activity, mentioning primarily male friends with whom they had played. This would seem to support Messner's understanding of sports as a significant arena for male individuation. Yet some informants mentioned girls with whom they remembered collecting cards. John, for example, recalled that his sister had been as much a collector as he was, and perhaps a bigger sports fan. He said that she lost interest in sports during her teenage years largely because of external pressures and constraints:

> She was in a situation in high school where she came along at a bad time. Because she always wanted to do girls' sports.... She would have loved to do all that, but there wasn't anything. And I really think that if she would have grown up in an era where that was there, she would still have interest. You know, it's like, all of a sudden it's like, you're beyond that playing-with-boys stage.

The "playing-with-boys stage" that John mentioned suggests that in his preadolescent years there was more fluidity and a less rigid structure to gendered relationships. It was only after puberty that sports and playing with boys became inappropriate for John's sister and, thus, that gender distinctions became a "line in the sand" one was not allowed to cross over. It was during their teens that most collectors recalled abandoning their baseball cards or bringing their collecting hobby out of the public eye to avoid ridicule.

Collectors often reported that collecting was something for kids and that it was not considered "cool" for teenagers. Tim recalled giving up collecting for these reasons:

> You go through a growing-up phase and you get to the junior high age. You tend to do other things and give up. It's more of a... obviously I don't feel that way now, but... at the time it was more of a childhood thing of, now you're moving on to another stage, or something.

Kevin, the clerical worker and dealer who, in chapter 2, provided a sympathetic rendering of children at baseball card shows, never gave up collecting baseball cards. As soon as he became a teenager, however, his hobby became more isolated and less connected to a network of close friends:

> It became individual in junior [high], in high school — '63, yeah. That's about the time your interest turns to girls and cars . . . dates and that thing. You don't have the cash flow, and you don't want to admit that, so that it becomes more of a closet. . . . well, I just didn't spend money on girls and cars. What little money I had I put into baseball cards.

Bob explicitly recalled being teased in high school for his interest in cards:

> Bob: I can remember I used to read a lot of baseball books, and I got a little grief from that when I was in ninth grade.
> Q: How come?
> Bob: Well, it was kind of strange. I played baseball all through high school and out of high school, I played on the team, on the high school team, and that. And the guy that gave me the most grief was the center fielder. I don't know why that was; it was kind of weird.
> Q: Sort of like, big kids don't . . .
> Bob: Yeah, big kids don't collect. That's not the thing to do. That's something little kids do maybe.

John recalled quitting his hobby when he got "into that peer pressure type of thing when people think it's kind of childish to collect cards." Like Bob, he remembered being ridiculed for collecting by his roommates in college who he said would "give me shit" for spending money on cards. Those who did not face this kind of teasing often linked the end of their childhood collecting to the commencement of heterosexual relations with women. Calvin, a fifty-year-old dentist, had a somewhat typical memory of why he gave up collecting: "I collected until I was fifteen, sixteen, and then I quit for a number of years . . . just other interests I guess, and I just kind of lost interest and got interested in maybe girls and cars and school and other friends and things like that . . . definitely a kid's thing."

Many adults who returned to the hobby well after their teens also reported feeling pressure to hide it from others. Like Kevin, Doug talked of keeping his collecting "in the closet," meaning he did not let many people know about it. Wes admitted that when he began collecting as an adult, "it wasn't something I bragged to my friends" about. For most of these men, collecting was something they associated with an earlier stage in life. Yet even though they reported that stage to have been defined by all-male relationships, they also discussed how returning to it was considered less than manly. This view complicates understandings that see sports only as preparing boys to be heterosexual, masculine teenagers. For most of those interviewed, baseball cards were part of a stage in life when gender identities were first being explored. Cards involved informal levels of play that were not directly monitored or controlled by parents or other adults, and that allowed levels of intimacy between boys not generally accepted when they became teenagers.

In his ethnographic study of high school life in a small South Texas town, Douglas Foley noted that for many youths the competition for success in romance led to the breakup of single-sex relationships as both males and females sought social prominence through dating. Foley observed that competition for partners was more destructive to female than to male friendships, but noted that even the boys he interviewed defined their same-sex peer friends as those who "hung out" with them, whereas opposite-sex partners were ones with whom they could feel comfortable sharing their hopes and intimate feelings. Those most likely to maintain more intimate same-sex relationships were those with the least social prominence: the "nerds," the "nobodies," the "homeboys" or "homegirls." Because these teens lacked money, good looks, or family connections, they did not succeed in climbing the social status ladder in romance. Yet they also had the least at stake in same-sex relationships and were therefore freer not to be "cool." Foley argues that the competition for social status within romantic relationships among adolescents, which is socialized within an American capitalist culture, isolates people from one another, objectifies needs for human interaction, and breeds loneliness (1990, 78–79). Foley's observations suggest that the desire to return to a symbol of preadolescent life such as baseball cards may be related to the alienation that teenagers experience during gender socialization, and that, Foley says, also characterizes adult human relationships, sexual and otherwise, in American life.

It is worth noting that most of the collectors interviewed came, as we have seen, from modest, working-class backgrounds and were not likely to have been among the most socially prominent members of their high schools, at least on economic grounds (see the accompanying table). Although it is impossible to determine exactly

Collecting Sets

Background of Informants

Name	Age	Occupation	Mother's occupation	Father's occupation
Barry	31	UPS delivery driver	Teacher	Electrician
Bert	31	Insurance agent	Homemaker/ newspaper columnist	Architectural engineer
Bill	42	Unemployed factory worker	Homemaker	Electrician
Bob	40	Pharmacist	Homemaker	Grocery store manager
Brian	19	College student	Nurse	[Did not live with father]
Calvin	50	Dentist	Homemaker	Salesman
Dave	39	Lawyer	Domestic/factory worker	Steel factory worker
Donald	40	Municipal employee	Homemaker	Weapons factory worker
Doug	39	Card shop owner	Homemaker	Auto factory worker
Glenn	34	University professor	Academic/writer	Academic/writer
Henry	40	Warehouse worker	[Did not live with mother]	Die caster
Janet	36	Homemaker	Teacher	Teacher
John	27	Marketing/sales executive	Homemaker	Excavating company owner
Josh	41	Card shop owner	Homemaker	Insurance agent
Ken	31	Commercial artist	Homemaker (worked for Ken's father)	Wholesale manager
Kevin	44	Clerical worker	Homemaker	Metalworker
Larry	31	Full-time dealer	Homemaker	Engineer
Matt	29	Graduate student	Homemaker	Manufacturer's representative
Norm	42	Corporate executive	Homemaker	Machine tools salesman
Paul	41	Lawyer	Teacher	Teacher
Peter	36	Card shop owner	Farmer	Farmer
Rex	26	Engineer	Homemaker	Builder/ construction worker

Background of Informants *(continued)*

Name	Age	Occupation	Mother's occupation	Father's occupation
Sam	28	Film production consultant	USDA field inspector	[Did not live with father]
Shane	37	Factory worker	Homemaker	Steel mill worker
Stan	26	Sales executive	Homemaker	Corporate executive
Steve	45	Part-time card shop owner	Homemaker	Blacksmith/ welder
Terry	50	Computer warehouse worker	Teacher	Teacher
Thomas	40	Candy company executive	Homemaker/part-time waitress	Steel warehouse worker
Tim	27	Junior marketing executive	College administrator	Mail carrier
Wes	33	Grade-school teacher	Nurse	Janitor/manual laborer

how prominent the collectors had been in high school, Foley's observations suggest that perhaps many, particularly those like Kevin who never gave up collecting in high school, felt especially marginalized by the heterosexual dating and status competition typical of teenage high school life in the United States. (Kevin explicitly stated that a lack of "cash flow," and his unwillingness to admit to it, contributed to his "closet" collecting hobby.) Foley's analysis also illustrates why so many collectors have gone underground with their hobby as adults or teenagers, not willing to risk ridicule or harm to their social status.

Although those who collected cards as teens did so against expectations of "normal" behavior, they did not necessarily return to the less structured sex roles of their preadolescent years. In fact, baseball card shows were a prime example of "male bonding," where, as we have seen, the only women who attended served primarily traditional roles as supporters of their husbands, sons, or fathers. The adult hobby was perhaps even more male dominated than the childhood collecting that informants often remembered. In terms of gender relations, this fact raises an important question: To what extent did the revival of this preadolescent popular culture form represent a desire of men to shore up gender boundaries by nostalgically recalling preadolescent gender socialization through sports, and to what extent did it represent a desire for more meaningful and intimate human relations? One way to address this question is to examine the kind of relationships that collectors formed in the processes of set collecting.

Many set collectors enjoyed shows as more than opportunities to buy cards. Shows also allowed men to encounter other men, to talk sports, and to revel in what one collector called "the commonality of baseball junkies." Tim, for example, said that despite the greed that some dealers exhibited, he looked forward to meeting people whenever he attended a show: "[At shows] usually you can just start talking baseball with [other people]. You know, it's kind of a fraternity-type thing. You could walk to pretty much any table there and most of the guys are . . . you could just start talking baseball. You have a common bond with them."

Tim's comparison of baseball card shows to fraternities is important, for it demonstrates the importance of gender to the "common bond" that he shared with other collectors at shows. Not only did Tim discuss the commonality at baseball card shows in male terms, but he also articulated how sports and baseball cards provided a context in which he could understand an almost universal bond with other men. Other collectors shared this sentiment, discussing the sense of "camaraderie" they experienced at shows. Barry explained how this sense could be integrated into the very individualistic act of set collecting:

> I love the shows. I could spend a ton of money at shows. I mean, there's always something that catches my eye. And I like talking to the dealers and seeing what they think, what's going on, and talking about old sets and tough cards to get, getting the best selection, especially when I'm trying to complete sets and I'm not that far away, and get there and somebody has the card I need.

If collecting sets allowed men to get involved in all-male social worlds, it often created boundaries between them and women. Collecting sometimes caused strain between husbands and wives whom I interviewed. In fact, collecting actually figured in the separation and divorce of two informants. Dave, the show promoter profiled in chapter 2 who had a conflict with the MCC, claimed that he was divorced from his wife in part because he was more devoted to his cards than he was to her. Calvin told me at the end of our interview that after he had recently separated from his wife, she refused to give him access to his large and valuable rookie card collection until it had been appraised and the divorce settlement had been finalized. In other cases the strain between husband and wife may not have been as extreme, but it was present. Sometimes set collecting drained family resources, both money and time, causing tension. Kevin cited this as a factor that eventually drove him from set collecting into dealing: "I was getting a little pressure from [my son's] mom. 'Now [that] you bought the cards, how are you going to pay for it?' So I tried to sell the old doubles."

Doug, who maintained his sets even though he owned a store and sold cards, described his wife's opinion of his hobby as lukewarm. Like Dave, he presented his cards as competing for his time, energy, and affection with his spouse:

> Q: Is this your first marriage?
> Doug: My only one, other than my baseball cards. It seems like I'm married to the store.
> Q: How does your wife feel about your collecting?
> Doug: She's tolerated it, I guess. She used to help me awhile back, but she doesn't anymore.

Even those who said their wives had no problem with their hobby also reported how they managed their collecting practices to avoid conflict. Tim explained that he did this by negotiating the finances of his hobby and controlling his desire for cards:

> [My wife] doesn't have any problem with [collecting]. Usually what I try to do, I try to put aside a certain amount of money on a regular basis so that I can just take that money and go to the show. Rather than take a paycheck and spend a bunch of it. So I try to budget it that way. She wouldn't be too happy with it if I came home with five hundred or a thousand dollars' worth of cards, I don't think.

I also encountered evidence that men sometimes used outright deceit to manage the strain their hobby placed on household budgets. One afternoon I was observing collectors in a baseball card shop called All-American Baseball Cards. A man entered wearing a suit and tie, looking as if he was just coming from work. He and the shop owner began discussing a display of cards that featured Detroit Tiger slugger Cecil Fielder. The cards were marked at twenty-five dollars each. The man bought them. As he wrote out his check, he said that his wife was going to think he had "gone nuts." The owner told the man to make the check out to All-American instead of All-American Baseball Cards; he said, "Your wife will think it's All-American Cleaners or All-American Grocers."

Collecting sets took up not only family income but also household space. Bob, for example, lived in a small three-bedroom ranch house with a walk-in living room and kitchenette with his wife, Janet, three children under the age of ten, and a dog. His already crowded living room contained a bookshelf for his collection and a card table where he sorted and priced cards for shows. Janet collected what are known as nonsports cards, or trading cards with cartoons, comics, celebrities, political figures, war battles, and other non-sports-related topics printed on them. Terry, the computer company employee and long-standing MCC member introduced in the previous chapter, turned the basement of his house into a mini-memorabilia archive. He mounted souvenirs and posters on walls and shelves, used floor-to-ceiling metal cabinets to store his cards (which included every baseball card set produced, dating back to the late 1940s), and had a personal computer for keeping inventory and updating pricing. Because an individual company set during the 1980s usually contained at least seven hundred cards, and because collectors often had sets dating back to their childhoods, collecting could potentially take up a lot of room in one's home. Steve, the card shop owner and Kmart stocking employee, discussed how he stored his cards at home. At the end of his description, he indicated his wife's attitude toward his collection: "I have them in books, the cards. I've got a room in my house there that we've got, our sports room. My sports room, I guess. My wife's not interested."

The barriers between men and women raised by their differing levels of interest in cards were as much a part of the gender dynamics of collecting sets as was the closeness between men that so many collectors reported feeling within the hobby. As with any other popular culture activity, however, the contradictions in baseball card collecting made the "bonds" among men within the hobby bonds of cardboard more than of cement. Most notably, the speculative market and influence of money on baseball card collecting were a significant source of stress among collectors.

Contradictions within Set Collecting

Although collecting sets may have allowed men to come into contact with fellow sports fans at shows, it also brought them into conflict with one another over issues of economic exchange. The monetary value of cards, particularly as cards became increasingly valuable during the 1980s, created stress for many collectors. Wes told how the value of his cards brought him into conflict with his wife at home:

> It came out a few weeks ago after San Francisco won the Super Bowl, about a Joe Montana card being worth $150 to $200, and my wife asked me, she said, "Do you have that card?" And I said, "Well, I've got everything since '73." And she said, "Why don't you sell it?" And I wouldn't have a full set then. And she can't understand, if you can get $150, [and] you spent $7 for the set, why would anyone want to hold it? I said, "Well, if I sell it I won't have a full set. I'm not in it for the money."

Wes's commitment to his set was more important than the money he would gain by selling it, whereas for his wife, the set's potential monetary value meant perhaps an opportunity to gain needed family income. Wes's story illustrates not only gendered conflict over the importance of sports, but also the strain that financial speculation placed on set collectors in the hobby. High prices for cards made it harder and harder for Wes to justify his desire to keep his sets. For many collectors the emphasis on trading and making money at shows made the hobby less "fun" and made collecting too much of a "business." For Wes, this tension had periodically driven him in and out of collecting for years. Rather than celebrating the fraternal bonds it evoked for him, he claimed that he had always been turned off by his fellow collectors:

> I didn't enjoy the people at all. I've never associated with people. A couple of my first experiences were with . . . I'd seen a kid going up with a 1963 Pete Rose rookie, which at the time was worth about fifty dollars, and going up to a dealer and the dealer saying, "Oh, yeah, that's an old card. That's not worth anything. I'll give you a half a dollar for it." . . . But the kid knew enough about it. And I

think that's where I got . . . I don't appreciate the dealers at all. But it was the only place to go where you could buy your sets. . . . I've gone in and out of loving it and hating it.

Doug, like many other collectors, interpreted his involvement in the hobby in terms of a jeremiad, and felt that baseball card collecting was experiencing a kind of moral decline. He said that at one time there had been a sense of community but that it had fallen away: "It's more of a business than a hobby. I guess it was always a business, too, but it was more . . . I guess there was a lot more camaraderie. You could talk to people about different things they were collecting. Now it's kind of like sell, sell, sell."

Collectors often blamed money for disengaging the act of collecting from a genuine interest in sports. If collecting was really only about financial speculation, then anybody could do it. Shane, a factory worker in his late thirties who collected with his son, saw this as a problem: "[Money] kind of takes away from the way the cards tie into the game itself. . . . I think it used to be a lot more fun when you were looking for particular stars."

A number of adult collectors felt that this sort of detraction was worst among kids who copied adult practices of financial speculation. Many informants complained that instead of being interested in cards because of a genuine interest in sports, or in a player or team, kids were interested only in cards that were worth a lot of money. Whereas collectors remembered their own childhood collecting practices as playful, they often saw contemporary kids as crass young business tycoons carefully placing cards away and hoarding them in plastic binders. Doug discussed how he felt the collecting habits of children had changed over time:

> The kids . . . a lot of them aren't really collecting sets, which is really kind of the backbone of the hobby. So that's changed. Now they just want hot cards. They want a card if they think it's hot. It seems like that's all they're interested in. I think that, to me, has to do with media hype. So they're not really looking at it for fun.

Ironically, although Dave chides youngsters for not being interested in set collecting, it was adult set collecting that initiated universal standards for cards that established their value. Contemporary children who decontextualized their cards, who feverishly searched for those that were "hot" and valuable, were only mirroring what they saw adults doing. Monetary value, an emphasis on condition, and a detachment from play with cards all stemmed from set collecting, which placed a premium on order more than on creativity, play, or even aesthetic pleasure.

One of the more striking things I discovered while talking to set collectors was how few actually looked at or enjoyed their cards after they bought them. Most stored them away and rarely looked at them again. Steve, for example, told me:

> I very rarely look. The only time I look through them anymore is if somebody stops by, a sports fan, and we look at them. Or occasionally something or somebody comes up, you know, "Oh, yeah, I remember." And you go back and look at it. But I really don't have them; they're just sitting there collecting dust.

Collectors were more likely to have their cards stored away in a closet, on a shelf, or even in a safe-deposit box, than to have the cards out in the open where they could look at or admire them. Because cards were not used in any tangible way, even collectors who complained about greed could articulate the value of their cards only in terms of exchange. However, particularly as inflation and speculation overtook the hobby during the 1980s, the emptiness of such exchange value became apparent even to many I interviewed. Wes, for example, told me that he was perplexed by the value of cards:

> I've been telling a lot of people that I think that [the value of cards is] going to . . . it's got to come [down]. It's cardboard. There's no value in cardboard. Topps can print up ten million sets, sell five million to the public, and put the other five million in a warehouse. . . . I've heard they even have the plates from the 1952 sets. They could print up as many Mickey Mantle cards as they wanted. Gold and silver, there's limited quantities. That's got value to it, but cardboard has no value to me.

Those I interviewed often felt conflicted about the relationship of money to their cards. Compared with other fan cultures, the largely male population of card collectors had a fair degree of economic power, so that a relatively large number of collectors were able to turn their fan subculture into a permanent source of income. The monetary value of cards helped to make the hobby seem more legitimate as an adult pursuit and less a childish activity. Although Wes saw the adult hobby as being overwhelmed by a superficial obsession with price and exchange, he also admitted that this obsession made the hobby more acceptable as an adult pursuit:

> Wes: I've never looked at [the hobby] in terms of value. But it's, I think, now it's a legitimate collecting, a legitimate hobby business. I think adults now accept it. And it's not anything that we have to hide and say, "Oh, I don't collect baseball cards."
> Q: Do you think they accept it because of the money involved?
> Wes: Definitely, because of the money.

This response speaks directly to the sense of ridicule many reported feeling as they collected sets after their preadolescent years. Monetary value made collecting a "rational" activity. Moreover, Wes also discussed how the commercial trade of baseball cards that arose from set collecting taught children beneficial values they could use in adult life. Although he expressed a common concern over the influence of greed upon kids who later collected as adults, he also felt that set collecting offered benefits:

> It will show [kids] a responsibility for collecting and taking care of, and not just buying. . . . My own kids will buy stuff and throw it in a drawer and it will be lost. And I see some of these kids who buy cards and save them. They protect them. And they're really concerned about it if it gets a bent corner. They're concerned about who they get, their organizational skills that they're learning . . . I've got one kid in this [second-grade] class who can tell me batting averages and where the person fit in the minor league. . . . For a second-grader to be reading that much, the reading skills I think are [very good]. So in that sense I do think it's good for kids. I think they are getting some values out of it.

Doug echoed many of Wes's sentiments regarding the benefits of collecting for kids. Although he lamented that children today do not have the kind of interest in the history of baseball that he said he did when he was younger, he also felt that the contemporary hobby taught kids some important lessons:

> I think it's a good collecting hobby and it's really good for kids. Now I think a lot of the focus on it, which the media has monitored too, that's what leads to the kids' "Well, how much is that card? And what will it be in the future?" . . . But I think it's a real good hobby for the kids to do a lot of reading. You know, I

think it's really beneficial. Plus, it's something they have that's well spent. If they do keep them in good condition it will have [value]. It's not like they go down to an arcade or something and blow five dollars on video games. And they have fifteen minutes of fun and, "Jeez, now I'm broke."

Janice Radway notes a parallel dynamic at work among the readers she surveyed and interviewed in her ethnographic study of female romance readers. They justified their reading, on the one hand, by claiming a consumer-oriented right to self-gratification, while simultaneously maintaining, on the other hand, that romance reading was edifying, productive, and consistent with values of thrift and hard work (1984, 118). Like romance readers, Wes and Doug affirmed the values of work in the way they praised the benefits of collecting for kids. Both discussed how collecting taught thrift, organization, and the value of education. In addition, in his comparison of card collecting to video games, Doug equated cards with the benefits of deferred gratification as opposed to the instant and fleeting sensual pleasures of consumer culture.

Further like romance readers, adult collectors founded their hobby on the pleasures and desires that emanated from their childhood consumption of a media artifact. The discussion of the benefits of collecting obscured the desires, fantasies, and pleasures that motivated their collecting as adults. Ironically, childhood play is often about evading the very forms of adult control over children's cultures that, according to Wes, baseball cards provide. What collectors told me and what I observed indicate that collectors' fond memories of baseball fandom had less to do with memories of learning to read, and more to do with forms of childhood play that served as a foundation for relationships with other boys.

Unlike the readers of romances that Radway studied, however, set collectors had a hard time discussing how their hobby was meaningful to them as adults. As we have seen, many collectors simply lost interest in the hobby when their sets were filled in. In addition, very few identified fellow collectors as among their most important or primary friends. Some collectors, however, used their cards as a means of expression and as a foundation for friendships. They tended to do so by breaking from the rationality of set collecting in one way or another.

Bill, an unemployed factory worker in his early forties, liked to collect "off-brand" baseball cards, such as those distributed by cereal companies or fast-food chains. Price guides generally list such cards at lower prices than corresponding cards from official company sets. In addition, Bill and some of his friends sought cards of players whom they had regarded as heroes when they were kids, but who had somehow been forgotten over time and who had never achieved the status of baseball "legend." By deliberately seeking cards that were not considered valuable or important, Bill's collecting practices conflicted with more rationalized processes of set building. He valued his cards more for the memories they evoked for himself and his friends than he did for their importance to filling in a personal set.

Sam, a film consultant in his late twenties, used cards in innovative and creative ways to express a highly ironic set of intertextual cultural sensibilities. I first became aware of this when he sent me a note on a piece of photocopied stationery he had made. He had arranged cards of Batman and Robin, and the Green Hornet and Kato along the top border. At the bottom center of the page he had placed the famous 1952 Gus Zernial card, which depicts the Kansas City Athletics slugger holding in one hand a bat with six baseballs nailed to it, while signaling OK with the other hand. The stationery was a sequence of visual non sequiturs layered atop one another. Even more than Bill's collection of off-brands, it lacked rational explanation and made these artifacts of popular culture look peculiar, even exotic. Sam's use of a particularly weird card like Zernial provided an ironic frame for these objects and placed baseball within the context of an intertextual media entertainment world, one in which images of sports circulated freely with those of commercial television programming.

Sam was an aficionado of kitsch, collecting as many forms as he could. He had an album collection that included recordings of Chad Everett singing, Robert Clary ("you know, Le Beau on *Hogan's Heroes*") performing at the Playboy Club, and game show host Wink Martindale telling Bible stories. Although he did collect full sets of baseball cards, he was particularly proud of those he considered "off-the-wall," including the aforementioned Zernial card. Sam conveyed his use of cards in an anecdote he told me:

> I'll tell you something that nobody else has done. We have, my friends and I, four or five guys: we have a Walt Williams card, a Gates Brown card, you know, from the seventies, Bob

Montgomery, and must be another guy in there now. Anyway, a while back we took a trip, and we had these cards, we sat these cards up on the dashboard. . . . So now, whenever we [or] somebody gets married, we take the cards. When I got married, they took the cards and put them in the back of the church and put them up. So then my friend got married out in Boston and we took the cards out there and put them up in the church, you know, when he got married. So they're like this traveling group of guys that, if somebody gets married, you take them and put them up there so they can attend. . . . They're all bent up or something, but I don't think anybody else does that with their cards. . . . So that's a good use for cards.

In some ways this anecdote illustrates the same gendered patterns I observed in set collecting. The cards are used to shore up male bonds during the weddings of Sam and his friends, events in which each made a commitment to a woman that usurped the commitment of the friends to one another. At the same time, however, the significance of these cards was much more open to interpretation than the significance of cards that are generally part of a set. The meaning of Sam's cards was highly contextual, based upon the history these friends had with both the cards and each other. Cards in sets, on the other hand, are rationally organized and understood within universal systems of value. Sam's ironic framing made the meaning of his collection problematic, whereas conventional set building involves the closing of a circle into an unproblematic whole.

For these collectors, baseball card collecting was a less solitary activity than it was for traditional set collectors. In fact, Sam explicitly discussed the value of his cards in terms of use rather than of exchange. The expressiveness of his practices illustrates, perhaps more than set collecting does, some of the particularly gendered desires that are so much a part of collecting in general. That is, to some degree collecting weird cards provided these men a more explicit context for adult, all-male relationships than did set collecting. Moreover, the ironic twist that Sam added to his collecting practices portrayed this context in a new light, reflecting an image of baseball card collecting that was less clearly focused and more subject to interpretation than that of more traditional set collecting.

Set collecting elicited a number of contradictory ideas and emotions in collectors. Although set collecting arose from a desire to return to a childhood hobby that collectors remembered as playful, set collectors sought legitimacy by focusing on order and rationalization. As a result, they created a hobby that made sense in adult terms but that also drained cards of whatever use value they had for kids, replacing it with the exchange value of a collector's item. Instead of drawing out the playful relationships they remembered having as children, collectors more often found themselves alone with their cards, collecting in ways that highlighted the most competitive and loneliest aspects of childhood collecting. Instead of being open and creative play, set collecting was more often about filling in missing pieces of a puzzle, setting the past, with all of its messy contradictions like scribbles on a card, in order.

The set collectors I interviewed were never really able to establish order. Yet the conflicts they faced between greed and nostalgia, manhood and boyhood, order and play are central not only to adult baseball card collecting, but also to the history of the adult hobby, its nostalgic orientation, and its relationship to baseball history. The next chapter looks at the origins of adult baseball card collecting and the implications of its nostalgia to the politics of gender and race.

4

Adult Male Baseball Card Collecting, Nostalgia, and the Cultural Politics of Gender and Race during the 1970s and 1980s

Of all the baseball card sets Topps produced between 1952 and the present, one of the most striking is the 1972 issue. Unlike the predictably banal fronts of cards produced in many previous years, these had bright orange-and-yellow borders stylized to look like a 1930s movie marquee with team names exaggeratedly printed on the top border as if they were emerging toward the viewer. Rather than picturing players only in stock poses with a "caught-in-the-headlights" look on their faces, this set featured a number of special cards showing players "in action." For the 1972 set, image was everything; Topps did not even indicate players' positions on the face of each card. This set was to baseball cards what Rowan and Martin's *Laugh-In* was to vaudeville. Their bright and colorful fronts combined the qualities of Peter Max pop art with Robert Crumb "Keep-on-Truckin'" T-shirts. In a word, these cards were "mod."

The image of baseball that Topps represented that year was of a game that was up-to-date, or, in the lexicon of 1972 preadolescents, "tough," "boss," perhaps even "groovy." Ironically, it was at precisely this same time that groups of primarily white middle-class men from across the United States were coming together at baseball card conventions to express their collective nostalgic appreciation of baseball cards. The last thing these men generally wanted their baseball cards to be was "groovy." Although adult males had collected baseball cards for almost a century, it was not until the early 1970s that

75

they first organized formally on any large scale.[1] Aside from meeting at conventions, they printed newsletters, bought and sold cards at flea markets and garage sales, and gathered in local sports collecting clubs. As they did so, they not only traded cards but also validated for one another that their personal pasts and memories were important, special, and meaningful. Each newly discovered collector confirmed once more that one was not alone, that others out there shared a similar past and an appreciation of baseball nostalgia.

From its very beginnings, however, the adult baseball card collecting hobby was problematic for its participants. For one thing, it was a boyish, childish thing to do, an irresponsible fetish for grown men with paternal responsibilities as husbands and fathers. As one collector stated during an interview, it took him several years to bring his collecting hobby "out of the closet."

In addition, collecting could be easily trivialized by its own participants. The hobby developed around consumer objects that kids had traditionally treated like money. Like kids, adults based their fun as much on trading, bartering, gambling, and hoarding cards as on any sort of appreciation of the cards. In the adult world, this translated into real money and real business. At conventions, one could not necessarily trust that another collector sincerely shared one's memories, fantasies, joys, and fondness for baseball. What might look to be a fellow collector could really be a con, out to rip off someone and make a quick dollar.

During the 1970s the most public forum within which collectors could communicate with one another about their hobby was newsletters. In newsletters, collectors not only revealed their nostalgic sentiments, but they also attempted to come to terms with the problems they faced in collecting cards as adults. Examining their attempts to manage these cultural tensions reveals some of the meanings and implications of their nostalgia as an expressive popular culture practice.

One of the most important events in the development of adult baseball card collecting in the United States occurred in October 1973 with the publication of the *Sports Collectors Digest* by John Stommen, a collector from Milan, Michigan. More than any other magazine or newsletter previously published, the *SCD* allowed collectors from around the United States to get in touch with one another, trade cards, and transform an individual, perhaps even eccentric, hobby into a subculture. All articles with bylines were printed with the address, and sometimes a photograph, of the author.[2]

Stommen issued *SCD* twice a month through the mail to collectors around the country. Unlike earlier publications such as *The Trader Speaks,* which consisted mostly of the ads of collectors who were auctioning memorabilia or seeking trades, *SCD* attempted to move beyond a newsletter format into one that offered more information and articles about collecting across the United States.[3] In addition, from its first issue there seemed to be a dual mission for *SCD.* Like other hobby publications, it served as a medium of communication and economic transaction among collectors and fans. It also solicited people who may never have been involved in the adult hobby to join in.[4] In his regular column "Our Hobby," Stommen (1973a) wrote in the first issue:

> "Sports Collecting—What's That?" You can imagine the quizzical person's mind at work when he or she first reads about the hobby or learns of it from a friend or associate.... sports fans—there are surely millions. But sports collectors—several thousand perhaps, maybe as many as 25,000. Quite likely, however, a good share of that number are still as yet unknown to one another.... we feel that bringing sports collectors in touch with each other is the chief function of a sports collecting publication and we are happy to join with the other exciting sports collecting publications in attaining this end.... In addition to serving current collectors, it is our intention to reach as many new sports collectors as is possible. We feel strongly that there are many, many people out there who would just love the excitement of sports collecting and our mission is to let them know there are many more folks just like themselves looking for them.

Toward this end, *SCD* reported on card collecting conventions around the country, local sport collecting clubs, and news about various sets of cards or archives of collectibles. It solicited letters from readers, as well as articles and advertisements. Readers sent in articles dealing with a range of topics related to baseball history and sports memorabilia collecting. To increase circulation, Stommen took out an ad in the December 14, 1973, issue of the *Sporting News.* He reflected an almost religious zeal in the following issue of *SCD,* writing to those who responded to the ad, "Welcome to the fold, folks" (1973b). By November 15, 1974, *SCD* had increased from eighteen to fifty-two pages. Advertisements increased as well. The December

31, 1974, issue contained five full pages of ads selling card sets and advertising auctions. By 1976, the total circulation for the magazine had reached forty-six hundred (Stommen 1976). *SCD* documented the growing popularity of the hobby by frequently publishing photocopies of articles about sports memorabilia collecting that readers had clipped from local newspapers and sent in.

Stommen's publication was a response to an adult baseball card collecting hobby that had been rapidly growing during the first years of the 1970s. Collectors in metropolitan areas such as Detroit, New York, Cincinnati, San Francisco, Indianapolis, and Washington, D.C., had begun organizing conventions by 1973. Judging from photographs of these conventions, the first adult collectors were generally young to middle-aged white men, a demographic core that would remain stable within the hobby throughout the next two decades. Conventions were usually sponsored by a local club, such as the American Sports Card Collectors Association (New York), the Southwestern Ohio Sports Collectors (Cincinnati), or the Mid-Atlantic Sports Collectors Association (Washington, D.C.). Clubs would rent a hotel hall or convention center for a weekend, charge baseball card vendors (or "dealers") a small fee to rent a display table, hire a retired or active athlete or sports figure to speak and to sign autographs, and charge an admission fee to collectors.

The *Sports Collectors Digest* covered this development as a hobby emerging among enthusiasts of all commercial spectator sports, but the focus of the publication was baseball, specifically major-league baseball. The cards, trivia, autographs, and memories most often reflected those of men between the ages of twenty-five and forty who grew up listening to major-league baseball on the radio or watching it on television during the 1940s and 1950s, and who collected cards as children.

In March 1974, *SCD* published the results of a popularity poll conducted by Sacramento, California, collector Wally Bryant, who wanted to determine the most and least favorite baseball card sets among the magazine's readers. The results showed that the highest-ranking cards tended to come from sets printed during the 1950s. The 1953 Bowman set, for example, was the top choice of those polled, receiving no negative votes. By contrast, the "swinging" 1972 Topps set was near the bottom at number twenty-five out of thirty-four on the composite list combining favorites and least favorites.

Further indicating the generational orientation of adult collectors in this time period, Bryant asked those surveyed about cards issued only after World War II. At the end of the column in which he announced the results, Bryant (1974) noted:

> I think despite the variety of contrasting opinions, a general consensus tended to be nostalgic with a disapproval of today's baseball card product.... Keedy [a fellow collector] perhaps said it best.... "[Topps cards] are getting flimsier and less imaginative each year. Turn back the clock!"

It is important to acknowledge that the collecting hobby did not necessarily speak with one voice on this issue. In fact, the 1972 Topps set was number three on the fifteen least favorite list *and* number six on the fifteen most favorite list. Yet the nostalgic orientation that Bryant recognized would become a central characteristic of the hobby during the 1970s. In that same issue, *SCD* published an announcement of a "flipping contest" that was to take place at a convention in Indianapolis. As collectors I interviewed remembered, children have long engaged in the practice of "flipping" cards as a kind of gambling game for the possession of cards. In a whimsical piece for the *New Yorker* in 1929, essayist Arthur Folwell recalled collecting Old Judge "cigarette pictures" as a boy in Brooklyn during the 1880s. He wrote how the adults in his neighborhood would give these cards to children who then "shot" them in a gambling game that contemporary adults would recognize as "flipping."

The rules took many forms but, in general, the game was much like pitching pennies or flipping coins. The Indianapolis convention organizers called for contestants to flip cards toward a particular point. The card landing closest won, with the flipper getting to keep all cards flipped (Flipping Contest 1974). Most important, the convention attempted to attract collectors and make itself seem fun by creating an event that nostalgically evoked images of boyhood play.

At the same time that collectors in *SCD* expressed nostalgic desires to recapture baseball cards they remembered from their childhoods, others sought to have baseball card collecting recognized as a serious and worthwhile adult pastime. Columnists and writers in the paper sometimes went to great lengths to establish the validity of collecting as an adult activity. One such proponent of card collecting was Dave Meiner, an enthusiastic hobbyist from southern

California. In 1974, to illustrate the legitimacy of adult collecting, Meiner published bibliographies of major newspaper and magazine articles that dealt with the topic of baseball card and sports memorabilia collecting. He noted with excitement that media coverage of the hobby had increased during the early 1970s. He also complained that even with the increased exposure, most sources of sports journalism still neglected memorabilia collectors. Meiner cited a 1969 letter that *Sporting News* publisher C. C. Johnson Spink had written to Ray Medeiros, an adult collector who had requested that the magazine do a better job of covering hobby news. Spink claimed that hobbyists did not make up a significant component of his publication's readership and therefore did not warrant much attention. Meiner (1974a) reprinted Medeiros's reply to the *Sporting News,* in which the collector wrote:

> There are thousands, not hundreds, of your readers who have no idea that anyone but themselves has a collection of sports material laying around.... You may wonder just what kind of people collect seriously. There are no "kooks" among serious collectors as one might irrationally conclude. There are some fine and respectable people. Men like Wirt Gammon and Bob Jasperson, sports-writers; Paul C. Frisz, former baseball executive; J. J. Smith and Lionel Carter, bankers; Mel Bailey, Air Force Major at the Pentagon; Anton Grobani, dentist; Ernie Harwell and Ron Menchine, sportscasters; Bob Solon and George R. Martin, schoolteachers; Charles Barker, an engineer right there in St. Louis.... There are many more. They were kids once. Now they're "serious collectors." Some have used their interest in the hobby of sports collecting as a stepping-stone to careers.

Like promoters of baseball throughout the century, Medeiros explicitly linked the "respectability" of collecting to the middle-class status of its practitioners. To further punctuate his claims to the "seriousness" of adult collecting, Medeiros strung together a barrage of rhetorical questions, including, "Did you know that a cigarette card of Honus Wagner is valued at hundreds of dollars?" (Meiner 1974a). Money and affluence may indeed have made the hobby of baseball card collecting seem more "important" and even "manly," but these factors also contradicted the playful nostalgia for boyhood that many sought to gain by collecting baseball cards. As collecting became increasingly prominent during the early 1970s, these tensions became increasingly pronounced and were articulated particularly as a conflict between nostalgia and money.

Such a dualistic understanding of collecting obscures important ways in which baseball cards were actually marketed consumer goods and commercial artifacts. Like other forms of mass media that emerged during the first part of the twentieth century, baseball cards melded advertising, mass communications, and popular culture. As cards developed over the decades, companies marketed them strategically to their consumers. For example, once Topps had established a monopoly in baseball card production and sales during the 1950s, 1960s, and early 1970s, it marketed its product to both fit in with and encourage forms of childhood play that very much resemble the baseball card "market" of the 1970s and 1980s. Topps would distribute its cards in series throughout the summer instead of all at once, hoping to create a sense of drama among youths who were trying to complete sets. Topps helped to turn these objects into a new kind of entertainment form. Cards represented a kind of graspable universe for kids who collected them, in that there was a finite number of cards printed that were difficult but not impossible to get.

In this respect, young audiences learned through their baseball cards not only about baseball but also about the rules of engagement in a capitalist market. Card collecting did this on two levels. First, it coaxed preadolescents into behaving as young consumers, teaching them how to spend money strategically on bubble gum packs and how to gain pleasure from the act of buying. Second, the very act of collecting implicitly meant that youths had become part of a "make-believe" capitalist market involving baseball cards. The nostalgic rhetoric surrounding baseball cards that has become popularized over the past twenty-five years has tended to portray these objects as meaningful in a mythic, eternal manner, disconnected from their history as commercial objects. Yet it is largely because commercial motivations are central to the traditions surrounding baseball cards that adult collectors for so long have bemoaned a contradiction between money and card collecting.

As far back as the early 1970s, sportswriters documenting the growing popularity of adult collecting complained about tensions between greed and nostalgia. Headlines for these stories emphasized the money that could be made selling baseball cards,[5] but often authors would recount their own nostalgic memories of collecting.

Such articles often grounded the experience of the author within the white middle-class suburb of the 1950s, and symbolically upheld baseball cards as representative of the "stability" of the nuclear family, as well as the "innocence" of children within it, during the early post–World War II era. The developing baseball card collectors market was presented as operating in tension with this symbolic understanding of baseball card collecting, even though it made the act of collecting "real" and understandable in adult terms. *Los Angeles Times* sportswriter Dwight Chapin wrote an article in 1974 that touched on these themes:

> I'm a 35-year-old addict. My habit is baseball cards, the kind you get with bubble gum at the corner market. . . . I got hooked as a kid one cold spring in Idaho, when the ground was wet and we couldn't go out and whack a baseball around. So we bought those little pictures of Stan Musial, Joe DiMaggio, Ted Williams and Jackie Robinson and pretended. . . . Some of us never got over it.

Chapin further depicted his playful nostalgic pleasures associated with baseball cards as threatened by women, children, adult responsibility, and ultimately an emphasis on monetary exchange:

> [Cards] had to compete for attention with wives and families and jobs, so it was a battle keeping those little pasteboards away from the incinerator at times. . . . then one day we discovered that collecting had changed. It wasn't all nostalgia, Buddy Kerr's batting average and Humberto Robinson's ERA, the smell of pink chewing gum. For some it was a business, like stocks and bonds, afflicted by soaring inflation. . . . Where have you gone, Joe DiMaggio and your Yankee pinstripes? To the bank obviously.

Similarly, a 1974 article about a Detroit baseball card convention quoted a promoter for the show, "a self proclaimed big collector," as saying he "would rather put his money in 'baseball cards than the stock market.' He says the cards are increasing three and four times in value" (Woodhull 1974). Yet the article went on to make a distinction between baseball card speculation and nostalgia:

> [Money] may be a rationalization, he concedes, because few men willingly part with their collections. . . . "Consciously, it may just be a love of the sport," he says. "Unconsciously, I'm sure for me, it's vicarious. I was never good enough to play. . . . It's also an unconscious search for order in life. You're always aiming to complete a set, and that's a sense of security." (Woodhull 1974)

A 1973 article in the *Cincinnati Post* represented baseball cards as symbolic of a past more genuine and real than the present. Once again, money was presented as operating in tension with the image of boyhood "innocence" connoted by the cards:

> Tucked away in countless attics across the country are shoe boxes, their cardboard sides bulging with neat stacks of baseball cards, bound by aging, cracking rubber bands. . . . Dog-eared and yellowed, forgotten . . . In those countless attics are the missing pieces of baseball card history. (Moores 1973)

The author of the article went on to say that "most collectors do not deal with each other in terms of money, but in terms of need; they prefer trading cards to making money purchases"; and he associated baseball cards with playfulness and youth by connecting them to images of "generations of zonked-out kids, white bubble-gum dust finger-marked on their jeans, flipping, trading, collecting their Woodie Helds, Warren Spahns, Bob Purkeys, Joey Jays, Jim Maloneys, Minnie Minosos" (Moores 1973).

Newspaper journalists were not the only ones who articulated conflicting values associated with adult baseball card collecting. Such conflicts ultimately destroyed Dave Meiner's relationship with *Sports Collectors Digest* and his public identity as an avid collector. Meiner's column was called "Sports Advocate," and its stated purpose was to serve "as an intermediary between disgruntled collectors and dealers or other collectors in an attempt to iron out differences" (Meiner 1973). Meiner's writing appeared in the *SCD* over a span of only about two years in the early 1970s, but in his columns he articulated important tensions that have operated within the hobby ever since.

As stated earlier, Meiner advocated greater publicity for the hobby in mainstream sports media and actively expressed a desire for collecting to grow nationally. Yet he also adopted a highly personal tone in his writing, as if card collectors shared a kind of metaphysical, emotional bond with one another. In a July 1974 column, for instance, he began with greetings from San Diego, where he and his wife were spending their vacation. He told how the two of them had not been able to spend much time together because of her teaching job eighty miles away from their home, how they were hoping to find jobs closer to one another the following year, and how they were enjoying their vacation together (Meiner 1974).

Yet Meiner's desire for the hobby to be a widely popular, serious adult activity was not always consistent with his attempt to use the hobby as a medium for developing meaningful interpersonal relationships. This contradiction culminated for Meiner in a series of articles in which he attempted to address problems that collectors were facing in trying to organize a national sports collectors club. In the first of these articles, he called for the establishment of a committee to form and set down a declaration of purpose, a constitution, bylaws, membership dues, and election of a journal publisher. He was angry that collectors had not been able to move past what he saw as petty infighting and form a national club. He wrote, "If we can enlist the aid of representative [*sic*] of existing clubs we can, with your help, all work together for the common good" (Meiner 1974b).

Meiner followed with six suggestions, each one a sort of manifesto about human agency and leadership: "Be willing to take a chance," "Get others involved in exciting, imaginative projects," "Provide new, refreshing, positive direction," "Get rid of the obsolete," "Put your ideas into action," "Set specific deadlines for each task." Each of these suggestions introduced a paragraph that conveyed that his article was about not only a national collecting organization per se, but also his own sense of alienation and frustration within the hobby. Under "Be willing to take a chance," for instance, Meiner (1974b) wrote:

> Look at the world with your own eyes, not with the eyes of others. Entertain and play with ideas that many regard as silly, mistaken or downright dangerous. If you are afraid of being laughed at or disapproved of for having foolish or unsound ideas, you will have the satisfaction of having everyone agree with you, but you will never be creative because creativity means being willing to go out on a limb, the person who would be creative must be able to endure loneliness — even ridicule. If you have a good idea which others are not ready to accept, there will be long periods of loneliness. There will be times when your fellow collectors think you are crazy, and you begin to wonder if they are right. A genuinely creative person, believing in his creation, is able to endure this loneliness — for years if necessary.

A sports memorabilia magazine might seem a strange place to vent in this manner, but this article illustrates the level of frustration that Meiner must have felt. In effect, he was urging collectors to grow up and act like serious, respectable citizens with a common goal rather than as selfish children. He expressed this sentiment in another column he wrote, titled "Inflation Rocks the Hobby" (1974d). In this piece he identified several "causes" he could blame for the rising prices of baseball cards that were forcing many fans out of the hobby. Among these culprits were "profiteers" and "young collectors with wealthy relatives." About profiteers he wrote, "This group always steps in when a hobby is hot. . . . they have no regard for ethics or anything other than the money in the pocket."

With the growth of the hobby, Meiner's complaints became increasingly irrelevant to *SCD* readers who, according to Meiner, largely ignored his column. Unable to position himself within the center of the hobby, and lacking an active response from readers, Meiner quit writing within one more year. He wrote a final column called "Reflections of a Departing Hobby Writer" (1975), in which he complained about apathy among collectors who were interested only in their own self-interests and were unwilling to make a commitment to other fans. After offering to give away his entire sports collection, Meiner wrote, "It's a sad commentary on humanity that we seldom do what we really believe in doing." He characterized once again those who did not share his perspective as infusing the hobby with "greed, me-firstness, one-upmanship, dishonesty and apathy."

In the more than two years during which he wrote for *SCD*, Meiner provided evidence of internal contradictions among those who initially made meaning out of this popular culture artifact. Throughout his columns, Meiner articulated an important tension larger than his personal perspective on the hobby. On the one hand, he wanted what many other collectors desired: a pleasure associated with nostalgically recapturing a sense of youthful playfulness through baseball cards and memorabilia. On the other hand, he wanted baseball card collecting to be adult, important, serious, and thus worthy of attention. His discontent reflects a larger problem concerning the hobby's boundaries that would plague the local collectors I observed. That is, although Meiner actively worked to make the hobby grow, this very expansion of collecting meant that its boundaries became vaguely defined, its meanings increasingly confused.

That money and nostalgia very early represented conflicting tensions in the hobby seems all but obvious. Yet focusing too much on this fact in some ways begs a central question: Why did increasing numbers of adult men during the early 1970s begin to find baseball cards particularly meaningful in the first place? What emotional and social needs did collectors want collecting to address, and in what ways did it address those needs?

Part of the answer to such questions lies in the historical, social, and cultural contexts in which adult baseball card collecting became an organized pastime. In an essay on popular arts in the modern United States, C. L. R. James predicted that popular culture would someday provide an "artistic comprehensive integration of modern life." Writing in the years immediately following World War II, James noted the various ways in which modern life in the United States conflicted with widely held notions of individuality. Socialization, lives regimented by work, the alienation of people from the mechanized products of their daily lives — all of these characteristics of modern life denied the individuality that is also widely celebrated within the United States. Out of the ashes of World War II, James saw the scale of social life in the United States grow to exaggerated proportions. He felt that under such conditions the integration of individuals with their society, and the various fragments of religion, work, family, and art that composed their lives, would become a necessity, "or the complexity and antagonisms of society will destroy the personality" (1993, 150–51).

James saw popular culture as speaking to the frustration and anger that people felt within a large-scale bureaucratic society. He argued that popular art forms could nurture desires for cultural expression, bringing people's collectively held need for freedom into open view. James further wrote that the eruption of such hopes for integrated life, expressed in real social demands, might also bring forth the suppressed "hatreds, antagonisms, [and] frustrations" of a society. James vaguely alluded to the frustrations surrounding class and race "eating away at the core of the personalities of the great masses in the free democratic society of the United States." The hatred and frustration that simmer beneath the surface of a society that denies individuality provide fertile ground for totalitarian responses to expressions of freedom, responses that promise a sense of integration and universality in modern life by denying, rather than celebrating, freedom of expression. Totalitarian culture offers a fantasy of an integrated subject located in a mythic past of solid traditions and "community" (1993, 158–63).

The adult baseball card collecting hobby emerged during the late 1960s, an era when popular culture became a fertile ground for expressions of individuality and freedom. The civil rights and antiwar movements had allowed vast numbers of the population to raise fundamental questions about the individual in post–World War II American society. The feminist movements, which emerged at the same time as adult baseball card collecting, positioned the family as a social institution rather than a private domain, and provided ground for women to express their desires for freedom. Popular music and art coming out of the youth counterculture expressed desires for alternatives to modern bureaucratic, mechanized society.

The expressions of baseball card collectors during this time period contrast rather sharply with those that emerged from such movements. For the most part, collectors were attempting to salvage a tradition rooted in baseball, a powerful national symbol. National identity has long been associated with baseball, which journalists called the "national pastime" as early as the 1850s. The celebration of a cultural practice centered on baseball had a particularly conservative resonance within the context of the time period in which it emerged. Yet we might also see in the hobby, as with the social protest movements, the expression of a desire for integration that James argues is suppressed within modern life. Meiner's articles and complaints express a strong desire for universality and an integration of individual and nation, as was illustrated by his desire to create a national hobby organization. As Fred Davis has argued (1979), nostalgic popular culture practices such as those surrounding baseball memorabilia collecting are of prime importance because nostalgia is more often a commentary of dissatisfaction with the present than it is an attempt to accurately understand the past.

Structural conditions during the 1970s and 1980s were particularly important to the dissatisfactions that many middle-class Americans felt. These conditions are especially relevant because of the way they disrupted expectations created during the 1950s for what middle-class life should be like in the United States. Beginning in the early 1970s, many Americans began to experience on a widespread level the consequences of what Barry Bluestone and Bennett Harrison have termed "deindustrialization." During the late 1960s, U.S. industries saw the beginning of a steady decline in the global economic dominance they had held since the end of World War II. As a response, they pulled back from the "social contract" they had had with organized labor since the late 1940s, busting unions, downsizing through cuts in personnel, investing capital resources in speculative ventures rather than upgrading facilities for increased productivity, and withdrawing most support for federal social welfare spending (Bluestone and Harrison 1982, 111–90).

Throughout the industrial Midwest and Northeast, manufacturers closed plants and moved their enterprises to the South, West, or Third World where labor was either unorganized or cheap. In addition, as plants closed and industries moved, corporations set into motion a series of recessionary cycles that cost millions of Americans their jobs. The economic cycles of the 1970s were characterized by a roller coaster of inflation and recession that impinged upon the ability of middle-class Americans to maintain a standard of living that they had, during the 1950s, come to expect as rightfully theirs. These cycles also made the Victorian, patriarchal, 1950s-style nuclear family an economic impossibility for many who had grown up in such households (Ehrenreich 1989).

By the early 1980s there had begun to develop a widening gap between rich and poor, and a shrinking middle class. Relatively stable, high-paying, unionized manufacturing jobs with benefits had been replaced by part-time or temporary minimum-wage, nonunion service employment with no benefits. A look at the employment history of the people I interviewed shows that many were directly affected by these trends. Each of the men who had become full-time baseball card dealers had earlier worked in relatively unstable service occupations during the 1980s (office garden and plant maintenance worker, freelance journalist, Kmart stocking employee). Some who had worked in higher-status occupations, such as one man who had been a computer analyst in a savings and loan, had experienced frequent layoffs and job instability. At the very least, the economic realities of this time made increasingly difficult the Victorian ideal of a man supporting his wife and children on a single family wage. Ironically, for those I interviewed who tried to do this, there was a strong burden on the female spouse to maintain a tight family budget.

Nostalgic desires within this context might be seen as liberatory in the ways they allowed people to grasp a sense of control over their lives amid unstable conditions outside of their control. More powerful, however, are the conservative implications of such nostalgia.

In the specific example of baseball card collecting, one can see that nostalgia feeds on a desire for safety and security located in a stable and mythical past. During the 1970s and 1980s, this nostalgia deflected critical attention away from the conditions and expectations of the 1950s that had helped to create contemporary problems. Instead, the nostalgic baseball fans I interviewed were more likely to lay the blame for social instabilities on civil rights groups, feminists, or homosexuals, who could be easily scapegoated as populations out to destroy the "family values" of the 1950s.

The aforementioned social changes may help to explain why a nostalgic longing for commercial entertainment produced during the 1950s and early 1960s became a core component of a more general commercial popular culture in the United States during the 1970s. The success of movies such as *American Graffiti* and *The Lords of Flatbush,* television programs such as *Happy Days* and *Laverne and Shirley,* and retreaded 1950s or early 1960s popular music and television stars such as Chuck Berry, Bobby Vinton, Annette Funicello, Frankie Valle, Chubby Checker, Tony Orlando, and Neil Sedaka were part of a widespread popular media focus on an idealized image of the United States during the early post–World War II era.[6] This phenomenon became known as the "nostalgia craze." Davis (1979) argues that the popularity of nostalgia reflected a quest for historical continuity resulting from a combination of life-course instabilities among the large population of young adults that made up the baby-boom generation, and broader historical discontinuities that were disrupting commonsense notions and ways of ordering the world. He notes that the nostalgia of the era focused a great deal on media images that were easily recycled to provide uniform constructions of the past.

The importance of cards to men who grew up during the 1950s and 1960s also has a great deal to do with the relationship of commercial culture, mass media, and entertainment to white suburban children. After World War II, the federal government sponsored policies that promoted suburban development, auto transit, and urban renewal. Suburban neighborhoods tended to be exclusively white as federal home loan policies, restrictive covenants, and redlining kept nonwhites from buying in new suburbs (Jackson 1985, 209–15).

These new neighborhoods were not only white but also separated from the public culture and spaces of urban neighborhoods. For children growing up in the uprooted, fragmented contexts of

American suburban life, entertainment and mass media experienced in the home provided a primary connection to the public world. The commercial broadcasting of television programming during the 1950s, which developed from the model of radio in the 1930s, was one of the most powerful cultural forces in the daily lives of suburban Americans. As Lynn Spigel has argued, television sold itself in part by demonstrating how it could bring the experience of urban public spaces, such as ballparks, into the "private" sphere of the suburban home (1992, 99–135).

This development led to problems of diminishing baseball attendance during the 1950s.[7] Yet it also allowed sports team owners to take advantage of new markets through television and commercial broadcasting. Part of the reason for the dramatic fall of the minor leagues after World War II, for example, was the unwillingness of owners, networks, and stations to black out televised games that were broadcast in regions with minor-league teams (Rader 1984, 59; Voigt 1983, 279). Baseball drew its following, through television, from wide national audiences and from new suburban communities of former urban dwellers who now lived far outside city centers in regions formerly dominated by minor-league baseball. In addition, team owners chased national television audiences, moving franchises from cities such as Philadelphia, Boston, New York, Brooklyn, and Washington, D.C., to new "markets" in Kansas City, Milwaukee, San Francisco, Los Angeles, and Minneapolis-St. Paul.

Baseball cards spoke to the needs and desires of children in suburbs who had become alienated from urban forms of popular culture and whose play was increasingly mediated by commercial culture. Design innovations on cards that Topps produced during the 1950s — the use of team logos; the incorporation of extensive statistics, cartoons, and biographies on the backs of cards; the variations between horizontal and vertical design; the experimentation with color and superimposed imagery — speak to the visual literacy of children growing accustomed to watching televised game broadcasts that brought the experience of watching sports into the "safe" and convenient confines of the home. Significantly, the 1955 Bowman cards, the last that Bowman would produce, actually framed player photos inside a wood-paneled color television.

It should not be surprising, therefore, that the nostalgic focus of the 1970s was very often on other forms of popular culture. The popular 1970s song "Old Days" by the pop-rock group Chicago referred to "drive-in movies," *Howdy Doody,* and, of course, "baseball cards." The film *American Graffiti* foregrounded the popular music of the early 1960s and media personalities such as Wolfman Jack, as well as automobile-centered cultural meccas such as the downtown strip and the drive-in restaurant. The characters in the television situation comedy *Happy Days* often spoke of 1950s television programs such as *The Untouchables* and television stars such as Sid Caesar and Milton Berle. Like never before, commercial culture was a recycled image of itself during the 1970s.

That adult men should look nostalgically toward baseball during the 1970s is particularly significant, for in this time period the meaning of the game was remarkably contested. Popular Hollywood films about baseball, for example, broke with the more sentimental, mythic themes of films from the 1940s and 1950s, such as *The Pride of the Yankees* (1942) and *The Pride of St. Louis* (1952). Films like *Bang the Drum Slowly* (1973), *The Bingo Long Traveling All Stars and Motor Kings* (1976), and *The Bad News Bears* (1976) used cinematic techniques such as realism to present the meaning of baseball as problematic. *Bang the Drum Slowly,* for example, presented in a remarkably unsentimental fashion the common motif of a dying baseball player. *The Bad News Bears* portrayed a girl as a key to the success of a Little-League team and painted the relationship between fathers and sons on the baseball diamond as ultimately destructive. *Bingo Long* illustrated the history of African American professional baseball during the 1930s, celebrating a rebellious barnstorming team and highlighting the centrality of segregation and racism in baseball's past and in the nation's history.[8]

Even within major-league baseball there were a number of important changes during the 1970s. The Major League Baseball Players Association had successfully won court cases against the "reserve clause," which had made players the property of the teams they played for and had banned them from negotiating with other teams on any sort of independent basis. As a result, players asserted more independence in their careers than ever before, and demanded ever higher proportions of team profits in their salaries. Numerous major-league baseball owners decided to move their teams from turn-of-the-century inner-city ballparks to new multiuse AstroTurf stadiums conveniently located off interstate highways. And teams such as the Oakland Athletics abandoned traditional flannel uniforms for softball-style pullover polyester jerseys and tight beltless pants. The Athletics' owner, Charles Finley, even suggested that major-league baseball create color-coordinated infields and use orange baseballs at night.

Baseball card collectors in *Sports Collectors Digest* often portrayed such changes as disruptive to their enjoyment of baseball. Many columnists, in fact, employed an antimodern rhetoric in this regard. Jeff Mortimer, a collector who wrote a column in *SCD* during the 1970s, was one. Unlike Meiner, he used his space more to contemplate the meaning of baseball than to promote the collecting hobby. In one column (1975), for instance, he nostalgically recalled his own boyhood memories for the purpose of criticizing corporate greed and exploitation of sports audiences. He wrote, "I do not like waiting almost a week after the end of the regular season for the playoffs to begin, simply because the network wants to snare that big weekend audience." Mortimer went on to reflect on his boyhood memories of playing hooky from school to watch or listen to World Series games and to contrast these memories with the relationship between baseball and television during the 1970s:

> I do not like starting West Coast playoff and World Series games at 5:15 p.m., an utterly atrocious time for baseball, so the network can soak advertisers for prime time rates. And I cannot agree that it is worth it "because more fans get to see the games." . . . It is a peculiarly American notion that it is better for 50 million people to see a baseball game in which batters flail at shadows and outfielders are blinded by the setting sun, than it is for 20 million people to see a game played under proper conditions. . . . the idea, as I understand it, is to determine the world champion of baseball, not to sell still more razor blades and cars to a public that already has too many of them.

In this passage Mortimer assumed a relatively elitist position, bemoaning a decline of "pure" baseball as networks aimed to please the masses. Yet in another passage he conveyed populist sentiments, contrasting major-league baseball team owners Bill Veeck and Calvin Griffith:

> Veeck has always put the fan first: his theory is that it's up to the ball club to earn the customers' patronage and I, for one, can't wait to see what he's cooked up to lure Chicagoans back to Comisky

Park.... Griffith, on the other hand, is the majors' most notorious
tightwad, the kind of person who would dive in front of a freight
train to retrieve a nickel that fell out of his pocket.... He called
Rod Carew "nothing but a singles hitter" at arbitration time, fired
Billy Martin after he won a divisional title, hired Frank Quilici
partly because he somehow thought another Italian manager might
bring the fans back, then fired Quilici when that cheap ploy didn't
work.... Now, after 15 years in which his team has been pretty
handsomely supported in the Twin Cities (especially considering
the quality of the Twins' play for a number of those years), he's
casting covetous eyes elsewhere again.

Mortimer's column in *SCD* is but one example of how collectors
were struggling to define the meaning of baseball during the 1970s
baseball nostalgia. In his own somewhat conflicting perspective, Mortimer provides an illustration of how ambiguous the symbolic meaning of baseball had become. Popular representations of baseball
throughout the twentieth century idealized masculine, Anglo-Protes-
tant components of a national identity. During the 1960s and 1970s,
however, such a narrow vision of America had come under serious
attack from Americans whom it excluded. In his 1979 book on the
baby-boom generation, journalist Landon Jones wrote a revealing
essay about nostalgia among this demographic group.

Jones portrayed this post–World War II generation as a large body
of the population that experienced key historical moments simultaneously. Coming out of an era he characterized as both stable and
prosperous, baby boomers were rocked by "the Kennedy assassina-
tion, riots in the cities, protests, the war in Vietnam, the counterculture, women's liberation, homosexual liberation, and the accel-
erating pace of technological change" (1979, 240). The disruptions
of "the sixties snapped something... within the generation at large
that intensified its need for nostalgia" (1979, 241).

What is most important about Jones's analysis is not the information he provides but the perspective he reveals. After all, the women's
and gay rights movements might not have been seen as disruptive by
many women and gays, and it would be hard to argue that the pace
of technological change was any greater at the end of the twentieth
century than it was at the beginning. What Jones expresses, however, is a particularly white, male discomfort with groups challenging

a stable, unproblematic core national identity centered on the authority of white middle-class men. His analysis is a prime example of the conservative orientation of baseball nostalgia, which makes it easy to lay blame for social insecurities on those who challenge the social position of whiteness and partriarchy. Within this context, Jones portrays baseball memories as providing a symbolic refuge:

> Why baseball instead of football? The reason, I think, lies in the special character of baseball during the fifties and early sixties when the baby boom was growing up. In those days, before the time of expansion and free agents, all the events of a baseball game unfolded in a single summer's night in only eight ball parks. At the beginning of the 1950's, there were sixteen major-league teams; at the end of the 1950's, there were still sixteen major league teams. Unlike the more volatile and technocratic professional football, baseball, in the fifties, offered a reassuring tintype of an unchanging world of small-town values. In baseball, the baby boom found the objective correlative of its childhood—stable, predictable, and timeless. The answer to Simon and Garfunkel's question—"Where have you gone, Joe DiMaggio?"—was not just that he was selling coffee makers. (1979, 242)

This passage is particularly striking, for it reveals a startling level of historical blindness. Between 1952 and 1960, six teams moved from one city to another, major-league attendance plummeted, and minor-league teams folded by the score. Baseball was anything but stable during this era. More important than the fact that Jones is historically incorrect, however, is that he is willing to overlook history and create an image of 1950s baseball as a transcendent national tradition, one he implies is particularly meaningful to white men.

Since baseball's inception as an organized sport, its promoters have tried to present it as the game of a unified culture and national character, an ahistorical and mythic symbol of continuity and stability in American life. Yet they have also controlled it monopolistically as a commercial commodity, not a public trust, and have done so in undeniably undemocratic and often racist ways (Levine 1985). For example, to maintain the loyalty of white middle-class fans, for more than sixty years the major leagues banned African Americans from playing the game, until Jackie Robinson broke the "color line" in 1947.

Baby-boom writers like Landon Jones who grew up during the 1940s and 1950s knew baseball after its segregationist policies had been lifted. However, those who promoted the game often struggled to maintain the centrality of white masculine heroism within baseball, lest they undermine its association with nationalism among white audiences that were already attending baseball games less and less frequently. Jackie Robinson's 1954 Topps card illustrates how, as an official representative of major-league baseball, the Topps Corporation attempted to present an African American hero in terms that were not threatening to white audiences.

Topps printed cards of both white and black baseball players in their sets during the 1950s. For the most part, they placed all players, regardless of race, in the same standard poses on the front of each card. These images seem to reveal an effort not to make "an issue" out of race. They do not celebrate African-Americans in particular, but they do not treat them any differently than European American players. The back of Jackie Robinson's card, however, blatantly illustrates the orientation of these cards toward potential concerns among white consumers.

The comic strip on this card contains two frames. In the first, Robinson is shown swinging a bat. The caption explains, "Jack is well known as one of baseball's top performers." The next frame pictures him in a coat and tie, surrounded by white children, in the middle of a radio studio. Underneath, the caption reads, "He is also known as the head of the National Broadcasting Co.'s Community activities, where he helps youngsters of all creeds." On the one hand, this card portrays Robinson as an African American success story, a role model for African American equality and integration. On the other hand, it presents him as a success precisely because of his ability to adopt to the terms of a white corporate culture as a loyal spokesperson for a large corporation (NBC). In addition, although the card praises Robinson for speaking to all children, it foregrounds his ability to speak to white ones without showing any animosity or hostility toward them.

Throughout its many changes between the 1870s and the 1950s, major-league baseball presented to its audiences an image of national identity that highlighted the centrality of whiteness and maleness. Its promoters and artifacts celebrated exclusively male bonds and communities, and promised never to offend white audiences. They did all of this while also staking out the unique claim as America's national pastime.

It should not be surprising, therefore, that Jones makes historical errors and reveals sexist and racist assumptions. He correctly understands that baseball nostalgia stood in opposition to social protest movements that expressed desires for freedom and individuality. In his writing, and in the actions and words of other nostalgic baseball fans of the 1970s and 1980s, baseball speaks to desires for universality through a stability and tradition that more diverse cultural expressions threatened to collapse. Yet history offers too many contradictions to accept unquestioningly the position of baseball, or anything else for that matter, as a symbol of national innocence and purity.

What is particularly significant is the fact that both a mass-media journalist (Landon Jones) and a hobby magazine columnist (Jeff Mortimer) expressed a sensitivity toward the changing representation of the game of baseball. For Jones this sensitivity took the form of an idealized portrayal of the game during the 1950s, whereas for Mortimer it took the form of a direct attack upon changes he was witnessing as a fan during the 1970s. As much as they wanted baseball to be an unspoiled tradition, these writers continually confronted the reality that for as long as baseball has been a national icon it has been inescapably tied to commercial culture.

The emergence of baseball card collecting among white middle-class men during this time is but one revealing manifestation of the changing representation of baseball. Jones's rhetoric, as well as that of other sports journalists and hobbyists, communicates a desire for baseball and baseball cards to mean the same thing to everybody over all spans of time and in any social context. Yet this mythic vision associating baseball with wholesome, "all-American" boyish innocence is not inherent to the game. Rather, it was negotiated out of a particular set of historical circumstances at the turn of the century and reformulated during the 1920s and 1930s, to communicate a narrowly white, individualistic, masculine vision of national identity. In addition, this understanding of baseball's meaning has been contested throughout the history of the game from both within and outside major-league baseball. The opinion poll in which *SCD* readers expressed their dissatisfaction with the cards of the present addressed not only issues of aesthetics but also issues fundamentally about the meaning of a media artifact that they had come to associate with a sense of collective identity. Their nostalgia, on a very real level, was a way of expressing a desire that baseball, and all it purportedly represented about the nation, stay the same.

Conclusion

Almost every American male collected, sorted, organized, and possessed these now-valuable relics (it was amazing how compulsive even slobs could be), and entrusted them, sorted and branded, to a closet. As we grew up—the big suburban generation, sons of World War II vets who did well as the American economy expanded—and left home, those closets filled with '54 Aarons, '55 Clementes, and '56 Mantles were cleaned out by our long suffering mothers, who, following the admonition of the apostle Paul, thought we had reached an age to put away childish things, but, in fact, to paraphrase our Lord, they knew not what they did. Out went the shoe boxes with their carefully sorted, branded cargo, out with jars of marbles and bales of comic books, out with all the flora, fauna, pennants, totems, and paraphernalia of childhood that we once couldn't live without and thought we'd save forever. Now, like the past itself, the shoe boxes and cards are gone; unlike the past, the cards and comic books are worth money. This is the Oedipal tragedy of the 1980's. (Salisbury 1989, 189)

The epigraph, cited from sports journalist Luke Salisbury, refers to a common cliché that circulates among baseball card collectors: that mothers throw away their sons' baseball cards. Salisbury's passage and the cliché to which it refers illustrate some of the undeniable ways in which the nostalgic orientation of adult baseball card collecting is intricately linked to ideas about race, class, and, perhaps most important, gender. Most scholars who have studied the relationship between sports and masculinity have observed how athletic competition makes "men" out of "boys," ritually and symbolically affirming the power and privilege of men in a male-dominated society. Although I do not deny the validity of these insights, they do miss an equally important way in which sports spectatorship addresses the gendered positions of its male audiences, one that is central to Salisbury's quotation: how sports make "boys" out of "men." Baseball card collecting has provided a rich context for understanding this fundamentally nostalgic orientation of sports spectatorship. It is within this kind of nostalgia that we can begin to analyze the complex sets of possibilities and limitations offered by the subcultural community of baseball card collectors I observed.

I use the term *community* in the previous sentence perhaps too loosely, for as the previous pages of observation and history have illustrated, collecting is far from a communal, mutual activity unmediated by commercial contexts and demands. Where a community could best be said to exist, at baseball card shows and in the MCC, collectors behaved in an antagonistic and distrustful manner toward one another as often as they did in an appreciative and respectful way. Yet to seek "authentic community" within subcultures of popular culture is to miss the many reasons that they are significant. More important are the desires for community, the needs for meaningful and playful avenues of expression to which subcultural practices speak.

One aspect of the interviews I conducted is particularly striking. Despite their narratives of disillusionment, greed, backbiting, and pettiness, collectors expressed a tremendous underlying optimism that their hobby could transcend a sense of loneliness they often implied that they felt in public life. Whether through promoting a show and organizing guest appearances by former baseball stars, organizing a club with fellow collectors, or simply seeking camaraderie at a venue of exchange, collectors placed a lot of faith in their hobby to provide connections with others that they did not experience either at work or in their homes. At the very least, this is evidence that collectors desire meaningful expression within and through their leisure-time hobby.

When I first began to work on this project, this desire for community was what I wanted to explore. I wanted to walk away from my study of baseball card collectors with an appreciation for the ways in which the practice of baseball card collecting nurtures the desire for respect and freedom that people are denied in their life choices and in their work. I am a sports fan myself, and I bristle when fellow sports fans are stereotyped as inarticulate and unsophisticated louts who passively crave violent competition. I am equally irritated with a snobbish elitism that places popular pleasures such as sports, soap operas, most other forms of television, popular fiction, and popular music on the "lowbrow" end of an arbitrary cultural hierarchy, particularly within scholarly communities that are supposed to be open and curious in asking innovative questions about the world around us. In my seven years of work on this project, I have been consistently amazed at the number of times fellow academics have brazenly insulted my research interests, almost completely unaware that they are doing so. These experiences in scholarly circles have given me a great deal of sympathy for collectors, who often told of feeling marginalized for their cultural tastes and preferences.

To some extent, then, I do appreciate the ways in which the collecting fan culture speaks to the daily life experiences of its members. However, I also walk away with feelings that are far more mixed, because whatever possibilities that might exist within the hobby operate in deep tension with its limitations. Within the field of cultural studies, it is most common to analyze the constraints of popular culture in terms of its commodified relationship to its audiences. But baseball card collecting revealed another related tension as well, that of the gender politics of sports spectatorship and sports fan subcultures.

Throughout this book I have drawn from the ideas of scholars whose work has established a dialogue surrounding the critical examination of sports, gender relations, and masculinity. Much of this work has come from sociologists of gender such as Michael Messner, who has examined the correlation between sports and prevalent ideas of male superiority and privilege. Messner discusses sports spectatorship in contemporary U.S. life as particularly relevant to men of high social status. He argues that sports experienced through channels of mass media are fundamentally "ideological," providing symbolic demonstrations of male physical prowess that support notions of masculine capability. As representations of male power, sports have become particularly relevant to men reacting against the advances and challenges of feminism and the women's movement (Messner 1990; 1992).

Michael Kimmel (1990) draws similar conclusions from his historical examination of baseball. He argues that at the turn of the century, popular media and institutional promoters offered the game to fans as a remedy for a perceived "crisis" in masculinity. According to Kimmel, baseball provided male audiences with empowering images of manhood that spoke to social frustrations resulting from alienating, docile, and disempowering forms of work. He characterizes the sport as part of a set of reactions to the way modern social conventions eroded traditional modes of patriarchal authority. Through male institutions such as baseball, the YMCA, and the Boy Scouts, men attempted to "revitalize" masculine authority symbolically, allowing fans both to resist what they feared was social "feminization" and to reunite male prowess with republican notions of virtue.

Both Messner and Kimmel illustrate some of the most prominent and important readings of spectator sports and their relationship to manhood in the United States. Each also suggests that manhood itself is a contradictory concept, as masculine ideals conjure up constantly unfulfilled expectations for men. However, the model of sports that these writers present is somewhat more static than their insights into gender. For the most part, they examine athletics as an agent of socialization without recognizing many of the complex uses and meanings that audiences associate with the sports they watch. If gender is complex and contradictory, is it not therefore possible that fans can create from their sports contradictory meanings, that athletics might speak to audiences of men and boys in ways that are less stable than Messner and Kimmel present?

Many historians of sports have held on to a greater possibility that athletics provides a meaningful context for cultural expression. They have often done so by examining the urban subcultural communities that created some of the most popular modern sports of the twentieth century. Perhaps because of this examination, historians have been able to explore some of the complexities and ironies that often emerge in the relationship between sports spectators and their audiences. Baseball historian Warren Goldstein (1989), for example, has written about baseball clubs that were prevalent in northeastern cities between 1840 and 1870, and has documented the emergence of professional baseball as a spectator sport. He observes how those who crafted the game's rules were practically obsessed with the issue of "manliness," changing the game's structure just to prove that baseball was not a boy's game but a man's pastime. In addition, a dichotomy between play and work in baseball emerged early on, paralleling the division between boys and men. Part of the enduring appeal of baseball to fans, according to Goldstein, is the way it has long evoked memories of childhood play. However, particularly since the inception of baseball as a profession during the 1870s, it has been structured as work. Goldstein argues that when people lament how the game has declined because of high salaries or greed, they are really expressing dismay at the discovery that what they remember as play from their childhood has turned out to be work in their adult lives.

Goldstein's analysis of baseball audiences complicates those provided by Messner and Kimmel, for he illustrates that sports spectatorship may have been meaningful for male fans in ways not anticipated, or perhaps not acknowledged, by its early promoters or by the men in Messner's interview sample. Goldstein certainly documents men using baseball to affirm a powerful, strong, and tough masculine persona, but he also illustrates how male baseball fans have enjoyed the game's evocation of boyhood play and have even expressed dismay at baseball becoming too "manly." Goldstein does not explore this contradiction in depth, but the existence of a tension between manhood and boyhood reveals the complex ways in which male sports spectators have used their games to understand their gendered identity.

Although he raises important questions about the relationship of masculinity to sports spectatorship, Goldstein does not place gender at the center of his analysis. Elliott Gorn, on the other hand, does take on this task in his pioneering work on bare-knuckle boxing during the nineteenth century. He traces the history of boxing to nineteenth-century ethnic "bachelor" subcultures that developed within urban areas such as New York City and San Francisco. Gorn ends his book with a reflection upon the commercialization of boxing in the twentieth century, noting how nineteenth-century boxing had been deeply tied to an underworld of oppositional and confrontational working-class men's amusements and culture. This subculture rejected Victorian norms of self-restraint and celebrated a physical masculinity. Commercial boxing, however, moved the boxing ring away from these communities. In effect, wealthy and middle-class consumers appropriated a working-class cultural form for their own amusement. Gorn sees such audiences as passive consumers who vicariously experienced a spectacle of "ultramasculine action" that spoke to the contradictions and deficiencies of modern middle- and upper-class manhood (1986, 202).

Similarly, Douglas Foley (1990), in his ethnographic study of a more contemporary youth culture in a South Texas small town during the early 1970s, celebrates what he sees as authentic working-class cultural expressions, such as those characteristic of a confrontational male Mexicano youth subculture he observed, in opposition to the deceptive and manipulative expressions of more socially prominent citizens and youths who organized their social lives around the celebration of high school football. He ends by arguing that even working-class participation in sports is misdirected, serving only to support the competitive, patriarchal values that perpetuate a system of class stratification and allow working classes to tolerate their own subjugation.

Both Gorn and Foley assess the constraints that commercial and even local sports spectacles place on the expressions of their audiences. Gorn's evaluation of boxing fans and their relationship to the kind of "crisis" in masculinity addressed by Kimmel, and Foley's assessment of high school football and its celebration of a particularly militaristic form of male athleticism, both illustrate the predominant ways in which sports provide highly polarized, exclusive, and prescribed models of gendered behavior. However, neither scholar addresses in depth the notion that commercial sports audiences may themselves read conflicting or even alternative messages into the sports they watch or enjoy. Although Gorn may be right about what boxing lost in its transformation into a commercial amusement, were there not also new possibilities created for fan expressions as fights became experienced within ever wider circles and increasingly diverse communities? And although Foley may accurately assess the way sports can attract working-class male audiences to a set of masculine ideals that are ultimately self-defeating, could this attraction itself be evidence of important contradictions?

The dichotomy that Gorn and Foley posit between an "authentic," working-class *popular* culture and an insincere, mediated *mass* culture becomes problematic in a study like mine. First, as I have discussed, within the context of the social world I observed, class was an extremely unstable and fluid category of analysis. This is not to say that class was not important. Indeed, class is an extremely important category for understanding any activity that takes place in leisure time. Classes existed in the sample I studied, but their boundaries were neither as clearly demarcated as they were during the nineteenth or early twentieth century in the United States, nor as they were in the small town that Foley observed. As Lynn Spigel has observed about class in the United States after World War II, "The category of class is difficult to pinpoint since its meaning is one of cultural identity rather than simply of income." In her study of television during the 1950s, she notes that many viewers may have imagined themselves as part of an upwardly mobile middle class, even if their salaries were relatively low (1992, 5). Second, the contradictions I noted in the collecting public's interpretation of cards, as well as hobbyists' struggles to locate "authentic" meaning within these objects, problematize the idea that one might be able to attribute authenticity or inauthenticity to any cultural form outside of the many contexts in which audiences understand it.

Baseball is a commercially mass-mediated spectacle; baseball cards are commercially produced artifacts and media forms intricately tied to professional sports; and adult baseball card collecting is a commercial industry driven by commerce and dependent upon commercially produced sports, souvenirs, and memorabilia. Yet the adult male baseball card collectors I observed were not passive recipients of the cultural life surrounding their hobby. The adult hobby was not created by the baseball card industry alone, but was largely a product of a fan subculture, one that actually caught companies such as Topps by surprise when it began to grow in popularity. Dismissing the hobby because of its commercial foundations discounts the important ways in which the collectors I studied attempted to make a mass-media form meaningful within their collecting subculture, and raises the difficulty of imagining any aspect of American life that exists entirely outside of commerce.

Subcultures and Cultural Politics

Dick Hebdige, George Lipsitz, and John Fiske have all explored various ways that people create, circulate, and appropriate mass culture for their own uses and effects. Hebdige has examined how, through style, working-class English music subcultures have reappropriated objects from daily life to reformulate or undermine their semiotic contents. In his analysis of punk culture, for example, Hebdige argues that style constantly disrupts meaning, expressing a kind of generalized "refusal" to make sense to the dominant culture on the part of those "condemned to subordinate positions and second class lives" (1979, 127–33). Lipsitz (1990) has studied how commercially produced popular music often is rooted in the subcultural practices of African American and Chicano/a communities, embodying expressions that have historically been employed in the resistance of race and class subordination. He has also argued (1982) that early post–World War II workers expressed their own aspirations for freedom not only on the shop floor, but also within subcultural communities associated with automobiles and working-class sports.

John Fiske also argues that all commercial forms contain contradictory meanings, some of which favor the status quo and some of which allow "disempowered people" to resist the dominant culture. Fiske even goes so far as to say that without resistant meanings, a commercially created cultural product will fail in the marketplace (1989, 1–7). Fiske recognizes not only the elevation of bourgeois values in shopping malls that promise to fulfill all human needs through the purchase of commodities, but also the desire of consumers, particularly female consumers who are "denied social power," to take control of their identity through performance and display, thereby expressing self-pride "in subcultural identities" (1989, 27–32).

Hebdige and Lipsitz celebrate subcultural communities as nurturing revolutionary consciousness. In and of themselves, subcultures are less important than the possibilities they represent—alternative ideologies or counterhegemonies that might emerge at truly revolutionary moments. Fiske, by contrast, is more optimistic about possibilities for resistance existing within people's everyday efforts to preserve their self-respect while adjusting to oppressive conditions. Yet, from my observations, the baseball card collecting subculture I witnessed did not fit comfortably into either of these models. It certainly did not nurture disruptive or revolutionary images, as do the subcultures that Hebdige and Lipsitz celebrate. And it was symbolically too oriented toward maintaining a status quo for me to completely accept Fiske's understanding of resistance within such popular expressions. Yet it was still a subculture that people created from their experiences with popular entertainment and made meaningful within the context of culturally significant hopes, pains, frustrations, and expectations that were woven into the fabric of their daily lives.

On its surface, baseball card collecting may seem too mainstream and conservative, and its constituency too comfortable, to ever be considered a subculture. One would not, for instance, quickly identify white, middle-class American men if asked to list disempowered and subordinate populations. Yet it is important to understand the ways in which even the men I studied sometimes felt stepped on and unimportant. The vast majority of those I interviewed worked in occupations that offered little or no opportunity for creativity or self-expression. This was not true, of course, for everybody. But it is important that my labeling of the men I observed as "middle class" or even "lower middle class" not obscure the fact that for every lawyer or dentist or college professor I found, there was also an insurance salesman, a warehouse worker, a clerical worker, or a factory worker. Indeed, most of the full-time dealers I interviewed dealt full-time because the jobs they had previously held had been unstable, unfulfilling, or boring.

The need for creativity and self-expression is not something to be taken lightly. As Stanley Aronowitz argues, it is a desire that is nurtured within childhood play, and when adults insist on maintaining a sense of creativity in their lives, it represents a profound form of resistance. Aronowitz notes how the process of maturation for most working Americans involves the acceptance of one's lot in life as a laborer or as someone whose work is subsumed within another institution's grand design. This means turning over great blocks of one's lifetime to an employer to do work that is profoundly alienating and unfulfilling. Work that is creative, by contrast, is both "self-generated and self-revelatory." Labor is the denial of creative work, wherein the greatest gift the worker can give to the objects she or he produces is discipline, obedience, and unquestioning loyalty (1973, 59–62).

In capitalist societies, play is the one area in which a child from an early stage learns that she or he can be creative and expressive. Like leisure, play is separated from work and family; self-generated play takes place apart from school or parental supervision. In school, children learn to endure boredom and to respect administrative supervision, qualities that train youths to grow into good workers and consumers. In play, on the other hand, children have a sphere of social life wherein they can express their humanity, their value as individuals. Aronowitz writes that "play is an activity that human beings create in which the person sees him- or herself in the object produced" (1973, 62).

Aronowitz contends that the strength people gain in play through peer acknowledgment of their self-worth can be a source of resistance against a social life designed to diminish their sense of dignity. As children grow, however, play becomes more institutionalized, and games are transformed into sports. As this happens, self-generated play is transformed into spectatorship, a passive activity that resembles work: it is neither self-created nor self-revealing. Nevertheless, the sphere of leisure remains for adults the "core of their self controlled lives. It is here alone that the chance remains to escape domination" (1973, 82–84).

On two levels, then, resistant strands might exist within the baseball card collecting subculture I observed. First, adult baseball card collectors have maintained a form of child's play in their adult lives. In this way, men's desire to become boys can be seen as a comment on men's work lives as adults — an expression within the maintenance of child's play of a refusal to accept the constraints represented by maturity. Moreover, because collecting involved, for many men, memories of play with childhood peers — trading, placing cards in bike spokes, playing Stratomatic, and so on — its resurgence in adult life might rekindle feelings of mutual affirmation gained when they had played with these objects. This adds a certain poignancy to the narrative of those who had collected into their high school years but felt compelled to keep their hobby a secret from their peers. Their continued involvement with baseball cards can be seen as a refusal to grow up, an attempt to maintain a form of play as a buffer against the painful denial of self that Aronowitz associates with maturation.

On a second level, collecting also can be seen as resisting the passive position of sports spectatorship. The collecting hobby, as was earlier noted, is not composed of mere fans; its constituents are active fans. The games adults remember playing as children with their cards demonstrate expressive and creative attempts to control their fan identity. Play in which children pieced together their own all-star teams, gambled for cards, or drew mustaches on the faces of players allowed young fans to generate their own understandings of baseball, to manipulate players, images, and statistics. On a much diminished level, adults also exerted a sense of control as they collected sets (particularly specialized or quirky ones), dealt at tables, promoted shows, wrote newsletters, and maintained clubs. The attempt to resist passive spectatorship reveals a broader attempt to wrest control over leisure and maintain it as the arena of playful creativity denied within the responsibilities of work and home.

To argue that there are resistant elements, strands, or possibilities within collecting, however, is quite different from arguing that the hobby itself is resistant or oppositional. Unlike the punks that Hebdige describes, baseball card enthusiasts tend to be obsessed with maintaining, not disrupting, a "symbolic order."[1] In fact, the aforementioned playful elements of adult collecting are often negotiated by collectors into a discourse about the monetary value of their cards. Contrary to resisting maturation, this process makes baseball card collecting a seemingly more adult and more "rational" or productive way to spend time. In addition, such a desire for control has extremely conservative implications, particularly, as mentioned in the preceding chapter, when placed within the historical context of an era in which nonwhite, nonheterosexual groups of men and women, in seeking their rightful place within American life, have implicitly undermined the stable social authority of white men.

The resistant possibilities within baseball card collecting operate in tension with another core aspect of sports spectatorship in the United States — the relationship of spectatorship to gender identities and ideologies. To see the hobby only as resistant is to ignore the central ways in which it affirms a very conservative orientation toward gender politics. My ethnographic and historical observations of baseball cards and baseball card collecting reveal a number of contradictions related to the gender dynamics of male sports spectatorship in contemporary American life, particularly contradictions involving the dichotomy between boyhood and manhood. Early baseball cards portrayed a game that was playful and fun but that also drew upon images that were serious and "manly." Later, baseball cards marketed to children portrayed the game as a boy's pastime played by heroic and paternal men. During the 1970s, adult men nostalgically returned to their childhood hobby of baseball card collecting, but at the same time attempted to make it seem worthy of adult attention. Collectors I interviewed and observed also remembered their cards as a playful part of their past, but in their attempt to make the hobby more legitimate and meaningful in their adult lives, they had separated their cards from these playful contexts and became dismayed when they saw children following their lead.

Because the relationship of sports, particularly baseball, to boyhood nostalgia has rarely been critically addressed, and because this relationship is at the root of so many contradictions within the collecting hobby, it is particularly important to analyze. Collectors nostalgically engaged with baseball cards within a larger media context in which baseball had long been used as a vehicle for mythic representations of national history. Film critic Viveca Gretton (1990) notes that popular American films often present baseball as a metaphor for both the American past in general and American boyhood in particular. Movies tend to present each nostalgically, particularly representing baseball as a symbol of authentic boyhood that is innocent, pure, and central to the national character. Gretton argues that films associating baseball with such metaphors suggest that the game has certain deep-seated, inherent meanings that have not changed and will not change over time. Ultimately, this mythic quality of the baseball metaphor portrays ideals of white male dominance by burying the histories of Americans who might be considered "marginal," and by elevating the importance of all-male relationships.

Contemporary baseball iconography offers infinite sites that illustrate Gretton's analysis of the game's nostalgic orientation, as well as illustrating the political implications of the historical amnesia baseball nostalgia involves. One of the most visible is the brand-new Oriole Park at Camden Yards, home of the Baltimore Orioles, which was completed in 1991 and was built to look like an old-fashioned, iron-construction urban ballpark of the years 1910–1930. When the Orioles are on the road, guides give regular tours of the park, regaling fans in the nostalgic splendor of the stadium. The guides present Oriole Park as "saving" the city and its historic buildings, pointing out that the large B & O Railroad warehouse beyond the right-field wall had been slated for demolition before the stadium design was approved. In glamorous terms, they discuss the history of the railroad once located where the ballpark now sits, and Babe Ruth, whose family's home and working-class tavern once stood somewhere behind second base. The quaint picture that the guides paint of the past is neat and unproblematic. They never mention that the railroad's history was fraught with pain, oppression, and struggle; how, for example, Camden Yards was the site of a bloody confrontation between workers, the militia, and railroad management during the depression of 1877, a confrontation that cost lives and helped spark strikes against railroad operators across the nation. Instead, guides proudly let fans peek behind the stadium's old-fashioned brick "facade" to see the technological fruits of modern life—a "state-of-the-art" computerized sound system and instant replay screen; exquisite luxury viewer boxes; and a prescription-grass field with a scientifically perfected drainage system—illustrating how "progress" can render the past and the present easily compatible.

What links the nostalgia represented in the architecture of Camden Yards, in Hollywood films, and in baseball card collecting is a desire to reestablish a sense of order and symbolic cohesion. Gretton's analysis of Hollywood film is particularly important because she associates this desire specifically with representations of whiteness and masculinity. She argues that baseball films tend to create a mythic formulation of American life that places the authority of white men at its eternally innocent core. Such representations may have been particularly meaningful during the 1980s, for, as was discussed in the preceding chapter, many white men experienced a real loss of power through deindustrialization during the 1970s and 1980s.

If the nostalgic orientation of baseball films served as a metaphor for boyhood innocence, thereby providing a cinematic representation of white male privilege during the 1980s, then might the nostalgic representations associated with baseball card collecting that were noted in earlier chapters contain similar implications? Salisbury's epigraph to this chapter, as well as the cliché it addresses, certainly indicates that such is the case. However, it also suggests that card collectors evoke relationships between gender and baseball nostalgia in complex ways. Salisbury uses baseball cards as a metaphor for the particular experiences of men in the baby-boom generation, those who grew up during the years immediately following World War II. As in Gretton's analysis of films, Salisbury universalizes the history of a middle-class, primarily white population ("the big suburban generation") as representing the experiences of "almost every American male." In a relatively typical fashion, he associates baseball cards with his preteen years, writing of his collecting hobby as something men left behind when they broke away from home as they marked out their identity and individual boundaries. Using an ironic tone, Salisbury accuses mothers who have thrown away baseball cards not only of thoughtless indiscretion but also of inflicting pain by severing a man's ties to his past (1989, 189).

An important aspect of Salisbury's passage is the way he blurs differences between men when discussing baseball cards and childhood. Salisbury represents the specific memory of boyhood collecting as an emblem of a universal bond among and between men. He further reinforces this idea of a male collectivity that apparently transcends boundaries of race and class when he posits the card collection in opposition to a woman, his mother, or rather the mothers of "nearly every American male."

It is certainly true that both men and women participate in sex-specific cultural activities, but this does not necessarily mean that such activities are the same or should be understood in the same ways. The image of "male bonding" so strongly associated with sports spectatorship in the United States tends to be elevated, on both symbolic and institutional levels, over most images of female collectivity. In a patriarchal culture, male bonding affirms masculinity, which in turn supports the viability of male privilege and dominance in public and private realms of social life. The idea of male bonding carries with it the denial of differences between men based upon an essential commonality defined in terms of its opposition to women. According to Susan Jeffords, the continual representation of male bonding in sports, beer commercials, and war movies constitutes an ongoing reaffirmation of the public world as masculine and the private, domestic world as feminine (1989, 59–62).

For young boys, baseball cards have long provided access to the masculine world of sports spectatorship. Cards may be seen as one of the ways in which a patriarchal culture was reconstituted for the generation of boys whose fathers' social authority was increasingly displaced by the authority of institutional education, mass media, the legal profession, and medicine (Chodorow 1978). Baseball cards, after all, have been images of male physical prowess and masculine "character," have been linked throughout their history to mass media, and have confirmed the heroic status of players through the

111

universal authority of statistics. Spigel, as well as male feminist media critics such as Joel Kovel and Fred Pfeil, have discussed mass media and consumer culture as establishing this kind of relationship with its young male audiences (Spigel 1992, 73–97; Kovel 1978; Pfeil 1990, 97–125). Each analyzes how media in the United States have long supplied symbolic representations of paternal authority for boys while also providing a context for them to establish their own gendered identity. Baseball cards have been a form of this media culture and have provided young audiences with a context for creating a gendered understanding of themselves.

However, for contemporary adult male collectors, cards also represent a material tie to the warmth and comfort of home and to memories of childhood irresponsibility and play, a tie that men clearly have shown a desire to recapture and, according to Salisbury, resent having lost. For many collectors I interviewed, boyhood was a period they remembered as being not only playful but also presexual. Just as collectors often blamed their mothers for throwing away their baseball cards, they often associated the end of their childhood hobby with the commencement of dating. This not only implied a shift in personal interests, it also meant a significant transformation in all-male peer groups. Passages such as Salisbury's and those cited in chapter 4 elevate preteen, all-boy peer group relationships to a mythic status emblematic of the "innocence" of boyhood. Yet such groups, and the fan cultures they form, are not benignly fenced off from the realities of gender and sexuality that teens and adults face. In fact, they are intimately connected to the rituals of heterosexual pairing, as well as to issues of gender politics, that become more clearly focused in later life.

During the 1970s, Angela McRobbie studied preadolescent working-class girl cultures in England, as well as the "teenybopper" fan cultures they shared. When McRobbie took into account the gendered contexts of these girls' lives, she found that their single-sex peer groups and fan cultures, often dismissed as unthreatening and conservative, formed a powerful culture for the girls she studied. These groups found ways to help one another evade work in school, where teachers attempted to persuade them to embrace a future of domesticity. Just as important, such groups provided a buffer between childhood and teenage life, when "the primacy of 'the couple' would de-

Conclusion

mand that these feminine activities and rituals be given up" (1991, 58). Similarly, pop stars such as David Cassidy provided girls with ways of exploring their sexual identity through fantasy without the sexual demands of boyfriends. McRobbie asserts that such youth cultures are not passive but allow girls within them to transform early adolescence "into a site of active feminine identity" (1991, 13–14).

McRobbie's insights into girl fan cultures illuminate the gender-specific nostalgia for boy fan cultures evoked within baseball card collecting. Boy peer groups, such as those that collected baseball cards, are a male parallel to McRobbie's teenyboppers. McRobbie's insights suggest that nostalgic desires to recapture such groups may have as much to do with sexuality as they do with class and work. Although the vast majority of dating and coupling rituals ultimately provide men with extraordinarily more power and control over their life choices than they do for women, many men actually experience their transformation into heterosexual subjects with a great deal of pain and confusion.

Perhaps this is why many adult collectors continued their hobby into their teen years despite the fact that many were openly ridiculed for doing so. Their persistence reveals a sense of loneliness associated with this stage of life. That is, at the moment of heterosexual coupling, boys who continued buying and collecting cards did not see the emotional value of their baseball cards diminish in comparison to the possibilities for romantic success. Instead, the opposite held true. As a result, they were abandoned by male peers in the competition for girls. The same boys who had been their intimate friends all too suddenly saw baseball cards as "kids' stuff."

Collecting, for these boys, became a solitary activity largely as a consequence of the cultural ties between male heterosexuality and fears of male intimacy. It is quite revealing that two collectors I interviewed discussed how as teenagers they had had to take their collections "into the closet." Perhaps the parallel to a metaphor for secret homosexuality is appropriate. Collecting may have allowed some boys to explore homoerotic desires, and to fantasize about masculine heroism and bodily strength, without facing the peer condemnation that goes along with homosexuality in high school settings. For others, perhaps it also forestalled the pain of rejection

113

and feelings of failure that define high school romance for boys. Collectors never told me that this was why they continued to collect their cards as teenagers, and I could imagine that many might want to burn this book for containing such a speculation. However, when understood within a larger context of gender and sexuality, it suggests a powerful reason why those who told personal narratives of "closet" collecting may have found their cards so meaningful. Fantasy is an important cultural source of pleasure that individuals can maintain in opposition to the world around them. Just as McRobbie's teenyboppers used pinups of David Cassidy for their own private purposes, so baseball cards allow teenage boys a way to stare at men in private spaces without the fear of being caught.

If this is true, then it might also be possible to conclude that the male bonding associated with the adult baseball card hobby resists the constraints of patriarchal heterosexuality by recalling a form of preteen boyhood fan culture. Yet male bonding is not the same thing as intimacy, and the specific ways in which collectors organized their hobby and remembered boyhood through their cards tended to prevent the realization of such resistance. For example, as we have seen, collectors often decried how money had ruined their hobby, making it hard for them to form meaningful friendships through their cards. Money, however, made the hobby not only profitable but also more serious, more instrumental, and therefore more manly. The same collectors who complained about greed often bragged in the same interview about the value of their cards. Yet money, in turn, made the hobby less akin to child's play and more like work: lonely, competitive, unfulfilling, and alienating.

To me, this contradiction suggests that the collectors I interviewed may have felt dissatisfaction with aspects of their gendered lives but were still, by and large, unable or unwilling to relinquish their positions as white men. The image of boyhood innocence prominent within the hobby further reinforces such a conclusion. By positing boyhood as innocent, one places a wall around it and takes it out of its cultural and social contexts, making it difficult to see segregated boy and girl groups as linked to the pain of heterosexual coupling. Instead, boyhood becomes a special world closed off to, and indeed hostile toward, females. Salisbury characterizes adult male baseball card collectors as recreating the "girl haters' club," and his description is insightful. It is easier for men to blame women for the pain and loneliness of teenage romance and heterosexual coupling than it is to blame a patriarchal culture and thereby to challenge one's own privileged position within it.

Rather than fulfilling needs for human affirmation, the practice of male bonding through boyhood nostalgia provides few alternatives outside the confines of patriarchal culture, offering only an idealized image of boyhood relationships. This is one of the sad ironies of baseball card collecting nostalgia. Not only does it white-wash the past and bury the histories of those outside the American "mainstream," but it also undermines opportunities for human contact that collectors seemed so often to seek, ultimately providing little understanding for much beyond the white, middle-class, 1950s-style patriarchal family.

I see a thin line between the nostalgic expressions prevalent among collectors and the conservative impulses that have drawn so many from this same demographic group to right-wing talk-show hosts, such as Rush Limbaugh, who have created a solid constituency among white men by espousing their support for "family values," law and order, and a return to the "innocence" and "simplicity" of 1950s America. Landon Jones's explanation for baseball nostalgia, quoted in chapter 4, equates social movements for equality with cultural disintegration, and baseball with transhistorical stability and continuity. When I see white men defensively proclaiming themselves victims of affirmative action and immigration, or indulging paranoid fantasies about the goals of feminism, or even arming themselves in paramilitary organizations to protect "their" nation, I also recognize a familiar current of nostalgia and desire for social order that can turn reactionary and ugly when it is defended vigorously enough.

This does not mean, however, that the possibilities for transcending loneliness in the public sphere went entirely unexplored within the hobby. Bob and Janet, the married couple whom I discuss briefly in chapter 3, engaged in parallel collecting hobbies that, in the context of their daily lives and marriage, seemed to constitute a cultural dialogue around gender. Bob, of course, collected baseball cards, but Janet, who had quit working outside the home after the birth of their third child, amassed an impressively large collection of nonsports cards, various trading cards that feature film and television celebrities, stills from movies or TV programs, politicians, war heroes, cartoons, pop music stars, and so on.

At first glance, Janet's collection seemed only to highlight her subordinate status as Bob's wife. She took up the collection seriously only after she had quit work to take care of the children full-time. Bob was generally supportive of Janet's collection, but hers received secondary status within the household. Both were members of the MCC (Janet being one of the few women), and at shows would set up their cards next to one another on the table. However, Janet did not often get much respect or recognition from the male members of the club. As she put it during an interview:

> Well, I'm involved with it [the MCC], but people don't really know that. They always think Bob does everything, but sometimes if we're taking reservations for a show — there are some male dealers who will not trust me to take the reservation for them. They have to call back and talk to Bob.

In addition, Janet told of buying baseball cards for both Bob and her son while trying to complete her own sets. She did not mention during our interviews whether Bob had ever reciprocated such a favor. On this level her hobby seemed to be particularly lonely. Her nonsports cards were generally not valued within the baseball card collecting subculture, her collecting energy was divided as she felt compelled to support both her husband's and her son's collections, and she was treated as a second-class citizen by the MCC. Overall, she assumed a traditionally nurturing position within her family's hobby, following Bob's lead in hobby interests, and perhaps even worked to maintain their relationship by doing so.

Yet upon closer examination there is another side to her actions. On the most obvious level, there were a lot of women who followed their husbands to baseball card shows, but not very many had a collection of their own to sell as Janet did. By doing so, Janet effectively inserted herself into the space of a show, and this gave her an active voice as well. When a collector would approach their table, she, not her husband, was the authoritative voice for the nonsports cards, something she told me a number of male collectors had a hard time accepting: "Somebody walks up to the table and says 'How much is this card worth?' and I'll tell them. And they don't believe me even though that's what the guide says, if I take it off the top of my head, which I can do sometimes."

Not only does this incident display Janet's competence in a hostile environment, it also shows that she was able to gain the upper hand in a moment of trade by exposing a man's irrational distrust of her for being a woman. Even though Janet was often irritated by such behavior, it is revealing that she said that prejudice against her among male collectors "is not necessarily a disadvantage or an advantage. It can be both." Moreover, Janet's collection often recalled moments in her life that paralleled those moments evoked for her husband by his baseball cards. She showed me Beatles cards that she remembered owning when she was what McRobbie might have called a "teeny-bopper." These cards recalled the gender-exclusive girl culture she remembered being a part of during her preteen years:

> We would trade the ones that we liked, if we liked a certain one. We didn't care to get all the numbered order. We would have . . . my neighbor, my baby-sitter, would come over with her packs, and she'd gotten . . . she'd like one and I liked another one, so we'd trade and that kind of thing. And then a girlfriend of mine collected the Monkees at the time, so we just kind of did the same thing. . . . Paul McCartney, that's who I liked. . . . I remember when we were collecting the Monkees with my other friend, we both liked Davy, so we were kind of stuck there.

If McRobbie is right that adolescent girl cultures cushion girls from the pain they experience as they begin encounters with boys, then Janet's nonsport card collection is an appropriate response and commentary on Bob's baseball cards. Just as baseball cards recall boyhood friendship groups for men, her Beatles cards nostalgically recall her girl-culture friendships as well. Even Janet's baseball card purchases for her husband carried a somewhat interventionist edge:

> It's gotten to the point, especially with some of Bob's sets, where I almost feel like that's part of my collection, too. I'll remember buying a particular card from a dealer, or I'll remember where we went. . . . We went to Wisconsin and we traded something for this card. And it's kind of gotten . . . intertwined sort of a thing.

Janet did not portray herself as just servicing her husband's hobby. By buying cards for Bob, she was able to make a claim of ownership over part of his collection. Throughout her collecting practices, then,

Janet subtly undermined the boundaries of male bonding so strongly associated with adult baseball card collecting. Her involvement in the hobby allowed her to negotiate her way into the all-male fan culture of baseball card collecting. She intervened in the exclusive process of male bonding by asserting herself at shows; countered the mythic status of boy fan culture by evoking her own memories of female collectivity centered on girl fan culture; and infused her own identity into her husband's privileged collection by purchasing many of his cards for him. None of this, of course, meant that either Bob or Janet transcended the gender-specific inequalities that characterized their lives, or that Bob necessarily overcame the gendered boundaries that characterized his hobby. But Janet's own collection and actions, and the critical dialogue she opened through her own mass-media pleasures, are reminders that cultural meaning is never impenetrable and that audiences actively negotiate the significance of their fan identities within the contexts of their daily lives.

Male bonding through the kind of baseball nostalgia associated with card collecting provides a largely conservative response to conditions of loneliness that many men may experience. Card collecting reestablishes divisions between men and women, and positions women as culprits guilty of sabotaging special, intimate male relationships. It idealizes a past predicated upon suburban white patriarchal authority and infuses warmth into a longing for stability and order. Yet even though I am critical of the male bonding associated with the baseball card collecting hobby, I must stop short of concluding that sports spectatorship in general, or even baseball card collecting in particular, can ultimately only perpetuate a reactionary longing for nostalgia. The very way in which adult baseball card collecting during the 1970s grew out of a contestation over some of the primary symbols associated with major-league baseball, and the complex relationships between boyhood and manhood that nostalgia evoke, suggest that such conclusions would be overly reductive.

When I think of my own memories as a sports fan, I recall major-league baseball drawing me from the narrowly conceived, affluent suburbs of San Francisco to the comparatively exotic world of Candlestick Park. One early May when I was about fifteen years old, I lied to my family and sneaked away from home alone, taking an intricate series of buses to see Vida Blue pitch against the Reds.

Those who remember the entirely unmemorable Giant teams of the 1970s may recall that the ballpark itself was often a lonely experience. (Some sportscasters used to refer sarcastically to the sparse crowds as "witnesses" rather than spectators.) What I remember about that day, however, even more than the game itself, was being alone in a public space and needing to share my experience with someone. As the game progressed, I found myself laughing and cheering with people I had been taught to fear, finding in a public urban space a world more plural and diverse than the one I knew at home.

Of course, my status as a male allowed me the privilege of being able to overcome my fears of others within a male-dominated environment like a ballpark. Indeed, perhaps I am only rationalizing the pleasure I gain from sports, and therefore my own complicity as a sports fan. My many ordeals at the ballpark were firmly embedded within commercial culture. My relationships with those around me were by no means unmediated, authentic, or noncommodified, and they did nothing to change the inequality of life outside the ballpark. My atomized suburban experience perhaps made me hungry as much for the spectacle of the crowd as for the intimacy of strangers. But my experiences as a fan also prepared me to think about the ways people are linked to one another's interests as human beings, to expand my understanding of "common sense" beyond the parochial and elitist confines I already knew.

A common hobby like baseball card collecting and its relationship to sports spectatorship illustrate the importance of how, despite the weaknesses of patriarchy in the home, sports remain a powerful component of popular pleasures that many men have a hard time abandoning. But it is also important not to dismiss activities such as baseball card collecting either as inherently reactionary or as trivial. Like almost everything else in American life, the hobby is guilty of perpetuating economic inequity, patriarchy, and racism; but no, baseball card collecting is neither a major cause nor an important product of these problems. What is most important about sports spectatorship is people's passionate engagement in hobbies such as baseball card collecting; the various ways in which even people who are white, middle class, and male feel marginalized and silenced as human beings; and what they do to resolve and address their frustrations. Baseball card collecting is a far way from providing a popular context in which people might express imaginative ideas and

alternatives to address their anger and pain. But so long as we recognize that submerged beneath people's popular culture is very often a common desire for human recognition, we can hope that someday the oppressive structures of our social life may in fact collapse
like a house of cards.

Notes on Methodology

The title for this book was inspired in part by Joel Kovel's remark about patriarchy and the nuclear family in the contemporary administrative state: "Bourgeois patriarchy is like a house nibbled away by termites: it looks fine for quite a while, but then collapses all of a sudden" (1978, 15). Unfortunately, as many discover daily, the old house is still holding up remarkably well. But this does not mean that Kovel's observation is entirely off the mark. This book is about a response by men to contemporary structures of patriarchal authority, a response that emerges from the competition and insincerity that characterize men's adult lives and often leave them with a lonely hunger for recognition.

I have interpreted the hobby of baseball card collecting as an expressive engagement with a popular, mass-media, consumer artifact. Cultural expressions can be understood as responses to social conditions in ways that render those conditions understandable and meaningful. Baseball cards, in and of themselves, are of no real consequence. What has made them important is how they have been woven into the lives of people and have often become emblematic of things larger and more profound than baseball games and bubble gum.

This study of baseball card collecting developed from another project, in which I interviewed participants in a major-league baseball open tryout camp during the summer of 1987. I found out during the course of that project that many of the young men with whom I spoke, all of whom were in their late teens or early twenties, collected baseball cards. During the spring and summer of 1988, I formalized a project designed to investigate adult baseball card collecting ethnographically.

Beginning in the winter of 1989, I began attending baseball card shows, sitting in baseball card shops, and taking notes on what I observed. In all, I attended twenty-one baseball card shows and auctions between the winter of 1989 and the summer of 1990. In addition, I sat in and observed five baseball card shops during this same time period. All but two of the shows and one of the shops were located in the upper midwestern city that served as the primary location for my research. The two other shows I attended were in the San Francisco Bay area, and the shop I observed was in Brooklyn, New York. I also observed and informally interviewed a baseball card dealer at a table he had set up at a shopping mall in Carlisle, Pennsylvania. I used my observations from these "out-of-town" experiences as a way of measuring what generalizations I could make about the hobby nationwide, and what ones I could attribute specifically to the Upper Midwest. At times all I did at shops and shows was eavesdrop and take notes; at other times I stood behind a table and helped a dealer sort cards or sell products, or I acted as a customer, buying, selling, and trading with baseball card dealers who stood behind tables.

In addition to participating and observing at shows, I conducted in-depth interviews with several hobbyists. I began my search for subjects at shows that I attended from January 1989 to August 1990. Initially I interviewed only dealers or those who were standing behind tables selling cards. Later I consulted those whom I interviewed for suggestions of others who might be willing to answer questions about the hobby. In the winter of 1990, I began distributing short surveys at shows in which I asked collectors to volunteer their names, addresses, and phone numbers. The surveys provided me with an additional list of possible interview subjects. Finally, I obtained from one collector an old copy of a local sport collectors club monthly newsletter that listed several of the club's officers on its back page. I contacted and interviewed several of those listed. As the hobby was overwhelmingly dominated by men, and because I felt there were strong links between sports, baseball card collecting, and male gender identities, I chose an almost entirely male sample to interview (thirty men, one woman).

Between August 1989 and July 1990, I interviewed thirty-one collectors and dealers. I chose to interview a range of age groups. However, since the central images associated with the hobby seem to be from the 1950s and early 1960s, I focused the bulk of my interviews on men who grew up during the early post-1945 era, commonly referred to as "baby boomers" (see chapter 2 for a profile of collectors). Nineteen members of my sample were born between 1940 and 1955, and twelve were born between 1955 and 1970. I also tried to interview collectors from a wide range of ethnic and class backgrounds. At least in the area of my research, however, there were very few nonwhite participants in the hobby. Twenty-nine of those I spoke with were Euro-American, one was African American, and one was Japanese American.

In terms of occupation, six of those with whom I formally spoke worked in, or were laid off from, blue-collar or clerical jobs, eleven worked in semiprofessional or managerial white-collar jobs (elementary school teaching, sales, commercial art, etc.), seven worked in elite professional white-collar jobs (dentistry, law, college teaching, etc.), and the one woman I interviewed, part of a married couple who together collected baseball and other trading cards, worked in unpaid household labor. The remaining six I interviewed sold or dealt baseball cards full-time.

Several of those from more privileged occupations had moved up the social ladder from the more working-class or less elite occupations of their parents. In addition, even many of those who did not move up in occupation had gained postsecondary education and degrees their parents did not have. Thirteen had experienced some degree of upward mobility, and sixteen had stayed in basically the same class position as their parents.

I came to each interview with a list of questions I intended to ask each informant. I did not rigidly stick to the list of questions, however, and would often pick up on important or noteworthy topics raised by the subject for the remainder of the interview. I would usually start interviews with a question such as, "What is your personal history of collecting?" or, "How did you become involved in collecting as a child, if at all, and how did it develop into an adult hobby?" I conducted the interviews at locations that were convenient for the subjects. Often, we scheduled interviews in the informant's home, but I also held them in restaurants, baseball card shops, a baseball card show, a factory floor, and outside a warehouse where a collector worked. I conducted eighteen follow-up interviews with sixteen subjects from my original sample. Each was taped and generally ran between sixty and ninety minutes. The tapes were transcribed by me and by Barbara McDonald at Dickinson College, and I typed out detailed notes from each conversation as well. As I have promised not to reveal the identity of the persons whom I interviewed, I have changed all of the names of the interview subjects, significant places, and local card-collecting organizations to which I have referred in this text.

Each quotation at the beginning of this book demonstrates a metaphorical understanding of baseball cards. The first two are exemplary of the common symbolic connections between baseball cards and idealized, nostalgic, and stable images of male preadolescence, particularly as located in the white middle-class home of the 1950s. Baseball cards are popularly understood as linked to a time in the life of a boy before he assumes a heterosexual identity in relation to women, when sports provide a context for relationships with other boys and for the gendered boundaries they will construct around their individual identities.

This particular symbolic understanding of baseball cards is important because it raises questions that help to interpret adult collecting as a particularly gendered cultural expression. Why would men be interested in representations of their preadolescent years, particularly ones that are exclusively male in nature? To what aspects of contemporary life in the United States is an activity such as baseball card collecting a response?

My reason for asking these questions is not to arrive at a definitive right answer, for when it comes to the passions and pleasures of people who engage in commercial entertainment, there are no easy answers. Instead, I see this book as initiating a dialogue about the gendered identities of men by critically examining an aspect of our culture. Baseball cards have developed over the course of a century into commonly recognized icons of American boyhood, and men have returned to these objects over the past two decades with tremendous fervor. It is precisely such activities, those which people care most about and feel are most important, that might provide the most valuable cultural contexts for such a dialogue.

Baseball cards are important for one other reason as well. They are an unmistakably commercial form that evokes all of the contradictory relationships of fans to a popular culture created around the dictates of commerce. This point is driven home perhaps most effectively by Alan "Mr. Mint" Rosen, the man responsible for the final epigraph. A former copy machine salesman from New Jersey, Rosen has become a national celebrity among collectors, claiming to have made more than $1 million buying and selling baseball cards. At the same time, however, many collectors blame Rosen for corrupting adult baseball card collecting by supposedly changing its focus from a love and appreciation of sports to an obsession with the resale value of cards. Whether one considers him a capitalist hero or a greedy villain, it is indeed ironic that the competition within capitalism, a value so central to athletics in the United States, could "ruin" a hobby built on the appreciation of sports. But in a consumer culture that divides human beings from one another, then offers consumer products to fulfill needs for fragmented human relationships that are left in the wake of such division, perhaps Rosen's sarcastic question is appropriate. Are not his actions what this nation is all about?

It has not been my position in this book to make the ludicrous assertion that men suffer just as much as women from patriarchy. In a culture, however, where male violence against women and against each other is so pervasive, where women still battle sexual harassment in the workplace and in the street, and where men still enjoy economic privileges over women such as disproportionately higher salaries and greater career opportunities, male identities are a problem and men must find a way to change. The fact that men are engaging in a cultural expression that speaks to their own gendered dissatisfactions at the very least suggests that such change is possible. Like chipped paint on the rafters in the house Kovel describes, it serves as evidence that the termites are still nibbling away.

Notes

Introduction

1. Not all series of baseball cards contained information about players' hair and eye color. This was a feature of the 1952 Topps set, however.

2. I come to this conclusion after speaking with baseball card collectors and dealers from regions such as New York City, San Francisco, and Harrisburg, Pennsylvania. All of these persons were involved in the hobby nationally, attending the biggest shows around the country. They confirmed that my observations surrounding the race and gender dynamics of the hobby in the Upper Midwest were not unique to that region. In fact, a collector in central Pennsylvania told me that he did not even bother setting up his table in malls frequented by nonwhite customers because, he claimed, white men are the only ones who seem to show much interest in collecting.

1. The Baseball Card Industry

1. A number of the collectors whom I interviewed got involved in the hobby after reading *The Sports Americana Baseball Card Price Guide,* retrieving their old cards, and trying to sell them at a show.

2. To produce and distribute baseball cards legally, companies must obtain licensing permission from the Major League Baseball Players Association, the players union. As long as a player is a member of the union, a company cannot use him as a spokesperson or represent him in one of its products without coming to a financial agreement with the MLBPA. In addition, if a card company is to represent that player as a member of a specific team, use a team logo, or in any other way use a franchise to sell cards and promote a product, that company must also come to a licensing agreement with major-league baseball. And, of course, companies must come to an agreement with each player they choose to represent on a card (Hailey 1986). (For a discussion of the issues related to baseball card company licensing related to the MLBPA, see Players Association executive director Marvin Miller's 1981

letter to the *Sports Collectors Digest* [Reader Reaction 1981b] and Franklin A. Steele's response to Miller's letter in a later issue [Reader Reaction 1981d]). New Jersey card producer Michael Schecter Associates (MSA), however, has begun to produce cards legally without a major-league baseball licensing contract by airbrushing team logos from photographs (Kiefer 1990b). In addition, legendary baseball card maverick George Broder has sold unlicensed, black-market cards called "Broders." These usually represent just a player's photo, with little or no writing on the front or back of the card. The cards are illegally produced and distributed, and dealers claim that major-league baseball has tried to shut down Broder's operation several times but has never been able to figure out where his production plants are located. Meanwhile, dealers keep showing up at shows with new cases of "Broders," claiming they are now produced somewhere in the South Pacific.

3. A company called Impel Marketing in Durham, North Carolina, now markets "pre-rookie" cards of minor-league players who seem to have promising careers ahead of them.

4. Members of subcultures often share in a jeremiad regarding those subcultures. Baseball card collecting is no exception in this regard, as its practitioners almost universally tell how the hobby has declined from its promise since they first began attending shows and buying cards. Even though there have been substantial, measurable changes in the hobby since the 1970s, it is important to acknowledge that such a folk narrative allows its teller to claim a certain amount of prestige within the hobby for having "been there" when things were good and for having inside knowledge of what the hobby is really all about.

2. Venues of Exchange and Adult Collecting

1. Two economic studies were done during the time period of my research, each correlating the significance of race to the price of cards listed in nationally sold commercial baseball card price guides. Torben Anderson and Sumner J. LaCroix found significant racial favoritism for white pitchers and hitters over African American players with comparable career statistics, but they concluded that the difference in price between cards of white players and Latin American players was insignificant (Anderson and LaCroix 1991). Clark Nardinelli and Curtis Simon, however, found significant discrimination against both African American and Latin American players. They found that cards featuring African American pitchers sold for an average of 16 percent less, and those of Latin American pitchers an average of 12 percent less, than those of white pitchers with comparable statistics. In addition, their analysis revealed that cards featuring African American hitters sold for 6.4 percent less, and Latin American hitters 17 percent less, than those of comparable white hitters (Nardinelli and Simon 1990).

3. Collecting Sets

1. Other researchers have also noted the centrality of set collecting to the adult baseball card hobby. These scholars, conducting their work within the fields of folklore and sociology, have noted the ways in which behavior among baseball card enthusiasts matches more general patterns of collecting behavior (see Belk et al. 1988; Danet and Katriel 1989).

2. Some companies produced more than one set during a season. Topps, for example, in 1990 produced its regular set as well as a set under the Bowman label.

4. Adult Male Baseball Card Collecting, Nostalgia, and the Cultural Politics of Gender and Race during the 1970s and 1980s

1. It is important to note here that adults did not begin collecting baseball cards in the 1970s. The marketing of baseball cards in packages of tobacco suggests that, in fact, adult collectors have existed for more than a century. Jefferson Burdick put together the most extensive collection of pre–World War II trading cards during his lifetime and, in 1947, donated it to the Metropolitan Museum of Art in New York. He also compiled a book, called *The American Card Catalogue,* that categorized each card he donated. For a historical account of adult involvement in baseball card collecting, see Kirk (1990), Clark (1976, 56), and Gannon (1990).

2. My research into this area is drawn primarily from back issues of *Sports Collectors Digest,* which is the largest current baseball card collecting trade publication. I have also looked at some back issues of another, older publication called *The Trader Speaks,* which was started by a collector in upstate New York named Dan Duschley in November 1968 and was eventually taken over by *SCD.* Yet it is important to note that small local newsletters and trade publications were printed all over the country in the late 1960s and early 1970s, including such titles as *American Card Collector, American Sports Collectors Herald, Association of Sports Collectors, Baseball Data Club, Baseball News, Baseball Press, Baseball Trade Hobbyist, Card Advertiser, Card Collector, Card Comments, Card Hobbyist, Card News and Comments, Collectors Digest, Foul Tip, Grandstand Manager, Hobbies to Enjoy, Hobby Enthusiast, International Sports Collecting Association News, Sport Fan, Sport Card Journal, Sport Hobbyist, Sport Collector, Sports Collectors Gazette, Sport Hobby Bulletin, Sports Collector by Perchalski, Sports Collector by Sugar, Sports Exchange Trading Post, Sports Journal, Sports Line, Sports Collecting World,* and *Zeb's Card Remarks.* These publications were usually put together by baseball fans who expressed their fandom through collecting and sought to provide a medium of communication with other fans. Some, such as *The Trader Speaks,* had audiences around the nation. Several collectors I interviewed first became actively involved in collecting with other adult men after reading such publications.

3. Between 1968 and 1972, the format of *The Trader Speaks* had also changed, but it continued to include brief, paragraph-length articles and a number of pages filled with classified ads.

4. Lisa Lewis writes that rock band fan clubs that produce newsletters similarly support an informal economy among fans: "Items of collection . . . enter this private exchange flow, as do goods produced expressly for fan consumption" (1990, 160–61).

5. For example, "$1,500 for a Honus Wagner: Face Cards with High Prices" (Woodhull 1974); "Collecting Baseball Cards for Love and Money" (Moores 1973); "The Card Game: Buy Low, Sell High" (Kelleter 1975); "Baseball Cards: Big Money" (Taylor 1975); "Ex-Stockbroker Now Deals in Bubble Gum Cards" (1975); "Gum Cards Have Withstood Time, Tight Money" (Tudor 1975); "Collecting Baseball Cards Can Be Serious Business" (Goldstein 1975).

6. I experienced this 1950s nostalgia strongly from 1973 to 1976 when I was in junior high school in Tiburon, California. Our school held an "American Graffiti Day," when students came to school dressed in 1950s clothing (boys in cuffed

jeans, leather jackets, and greased-back hair; girls in hoopskirts, saddle shoes, and ponytails) and danced at a "sock hop" in the gym during lunch hour. In conversations with individuals who went to junior high school at the same time as I did, I heard of similar events taking place in southern California, Ohio, and New York.

7. During the 1950s, major-league baseball faced the prospect of becoming an anachronistic urban relic. After a brief boom in the late 1940s, professional baseball team owners began to run into trouble. By 1956, major-league baseball attendance had dropped to one-third of its 1948 record-high levels. Minor-league attendance also fell, from 42 million in 1949 to 15 million in 1957 (Rader 1984, 33–60). Expenditures by sports spectators in general dropped from $282.2 million between 1947 and 1949, to only $252.4 million for the entire decade of the 1950s.

8. Viveca Gretton (1990) provides an excellent discussion of the symbolic representation of race, national identity, and gender in baseball films. See also Gary E. Dickerson's book (1991) on the history of Hollywood baseball films.

Conclusion

1. Hebdige distinguishes his use of this term from the Lacanian term often used in feminist psychoanalytic media criticism. His is a broader definition referring to the arrangement and understanding of cultural symbols in a society in a way that gives that society and the universe surrounding it an appearance of unity and coherence. Although baseball card collectors do take an object from childhood and disrupt its symbolic connotations by bringing it into adult contexts, they most often are struggling to reformulate a symbolic order rather than to undermine or subvert one (1979, 90).

References

Ambrosius, Greg. 1990a. Dealers. *Baseball Card Boom,* February, 98.
———. 1990b. Score. *Baseball Card Boom,* February, 94.
———. 1990c. Upper Deck. *Baseball Card Boom,* February, 34.
Anderson, Torben, and Sumner J. LaCroix. 1991. Customer Racial Discrimination in Major League Baseball. *Economic Inquiry* 29: 665–77.
Angell, Roger. 1984. *Late Innings: A Baseball Companion.* New York: Ballantine Books.
Aronowitz, Stanley. 1973. *False Promises: The Shaping of American Working Class Consciousness.* New York: McGraw-Hill.
Belk, Russell W., Melanie Wallendorf, John Sherry, Morris Holbrook, and Scott Roberts. 1988. Collectors and Collecting. *Advances in Consumer Research* 15: 548–53.
Bluestone, Barry, and Bennett Harrison. 1982. *The Deindustrialization of America: Plant Closings, Community Abandonment, and the Dismantling of Basic Industry.* New York: Basic Books.
Boyd, Brendan, and Frederick Harris. 1973. *The Great American Baseball Card Flipping, Trading, and Bubble Gum Book.* New York: Warner Paperback Books.
Bray, Cathy. 1983. Sport, Capitalism, and Patriarchy. *Canadian Woman Studies* 4(3): 11–13.
Bryant, Wally. 1974. 1953 Bowman Baseball Set Ranked First in Bryant's Popularity Poll. *Sports Collectors Digest.* March 15, 2.
Bryson, Lois. 1987. Sport and the Maintenance of Masculine Hegemony. *Women's Studies International Forum* 10, 349–60.
Butler, Don. 1990. Proliferation: A Flood of Shows Becomes an Ocean. *Baseball Card Boom,* February, 100.
Chapin, Dwight. 1974. Honus Wagner, My Wife, and Me. *Sports Collectors Digest,* August 31. First published in *Los Angeles Times.*

References

Chodorow, Nancy. 1978. *The Reproduction of Mothering: Psychoanalysis and the Sociology of Gender.* Berkeley: University of California Press.

Clark, Steve. 1976. *The Complete Book of Baseball Cards: For the Collector, Flipper, and Fan.* New York: Grosset and Dunlap.

Clifford, James, and George E. Marcus, eds. 1986. *Writing Culture: The Poetics and Politics of Ethnography.* Berkeley: University of California Press.

Danet, Brenda, and Tamar Katriel. 1989. No Two Alike: Play and Aesthetics in Collecting. *Play and Culture* 3: 227–53.

Davis, Fred. 1979. *Yearning for Yesterday: A Sociology of Nostalgia.* New York: Free Press.

Dickerson, Gary E. 1991. *The Cinema of Baseball: Images of America, 1929–1989.* Westport, Conn.: Meckler.

Ehrenreich, Barbara. 1989. *Fear of Falling: The Inner Life of the Middle Class.* New York: Pantheon Books.

Ellingboe, Steve. 1990. Interview by author. Iola, Wis., May 29.

Ex-stockbroker Now Deals in Bubble Gum Cards. 1975. *Detroit News,* April 24.

Fiske, John. 1989. *Reading the Popular.* Boston: Unwin Hyman.

Flipping Contest in Indianapolis. 1974. *Sports Collectors Digest,* March 15, 9.

Foley, Douglas. 1990. *Learning Capitalist Culture: Deep in the Heart of Tejas.* Philadelphia: University of Pennsylvania Press.

Gaines, Jane M. 1991. *Contested Culture: The Image, the Voice, and the Law.* Chapel Hill: University of North Carolina Press.

Gannon, Frank. 1990. Cards. *New Yorker,* August 13, 26–27.

Garr, Doug. 1990. Out of the Ball Park. *Business Week Assets,* June 15, 18.

Giamatti, A. Bartlett. 1990. *Take Time for Paradise: Americans and Their Games.* New York: Summit Books.

Goldstein, Allan. 1975. Collecting Baseball Cards Can Be Serious Business. *Baltimore Sun,* April 27.

Goldstein, Warren. 1989. *Playing for Keeps: A History of Early Baseball.* Ithaca, N.Y.: Cornell University Press.

Gorn, Elliott J. 1986. *The Manly Art: Bare-Knuckle Prize Fighting in America.* Ithaca, N.Y.: Cornell University Press.

Green, Paul. 1986. Guess Who's Joining the Hobby? *Sports Collectors Digest,* October 24, 56.

Gretton, Viveca. 1990. You Could Look It Up: Notes toward a Reading of Baseball, History, and Ideology in the Dominant Cinema. *CineAction!* 19 (summer/fall): 70–75.

Hailey, George D. 1986. Topps, MLBPA May Have Reached Agreement. *Sports Collectors Digest,* November 7, 50.

Hebdige, Dick. 1979. *Subculture: The Meaning of Style.* London: Methuen.

I Will Swap You a '52 Mickey Mantle for Your '85 Buick. 1990. *Wall Street Journal,* May 11.

Jackson, Kenneth T. 1985. *Crabgrass Frontier: The Suburbanization of the United States.* New York: Oxford University Press.

Jakubovics, Jerry. 1989. Management in Practice. Topps: Top Gum. *Management Review,* July, 14–16.

James, C. L. R. 1993. Popular Arts and Modern Society. In *American Civilization,* edited by Anna Grimshaw and Keith Hart. Cambridge, Mass.: Blackwell.

References

Jannings, Dana Andrew. 1989. Forget That '52 Mantle Card: "New Stuff" Has the Industry Booming. *Wall Street Journal,* April 21.

Jeffords, Susan. 1989. *The Remasculinization of America: Gender and the Vietnam War.* Bloomington: Indiana University Press.

Jenkins, Henry. 1992. *Textual Poachers: Television Fans and Participatory Culture.* New York: Routledge.

Jones, Landon Y. 1979. *Great Expectations: America and the Baby Boom Generation.* New York: Coward, McCann and Geoghegan.

Kelleter, Robert. 1975. The Card Game: Buy Low, Sell High. *Washington Post,* May 27.

Kiefer, Kit. 1990a. Alan Rosen. *Baseball Card Boom,* February, 108.

———. 1990b. Explosion. *Baseball Card Boom,* February, 142.

Kimmel, Michael S. 1990. Baseball and the Reconstruction of American Masculinity. In *Sport, Men, and the Gender Order: Critical Feminist Perspectives,* edited by Michael A. Messner and Donald Sabo, 55–65. Champaign, Ill.: Human Kinetics Press.

Kinsella, W. P. 1982. *Shoeless Joe.* New York: Ballantine Books.

Kirk, Troy. 1990. *Collector's Guide to Baseball Cards.* Radnor, Pa.: Wallace-Homestead.

Kovel, Joel. 1978. Rationalization of the Family. *Telos* 37 (fall): 5–21.

Krause Publications. 1989. *Annual Report,* 8–9.

Landsbaum, Mark. 1990. Publisher Scores with Designer Baseball Cards. *Los Angeles Times,* March 27.

Larson, Mark. 1990. 1980. *Baseball Card Boom,* February, 22–23.

Lasch, Christopher. 1978. *The Culture of Narcissism: American Life in an Age of Diminishing Expectations.* New York: W. W. Norton.

Lemke, Bob. 1981. The Coach's Box. *Sports Collectors Digest,* September 20, 4.

———. 1986. Hobby Hot Spell Raises Temperatures. *Sports Collectors Digest,* October 24, 76.

Lever, Janet. 1976. Sex Differences in the Games Children Play. *Social Problems* 23: 478–87.

Levine, Peter. 1985. *A. G. Spalding and the Rise of American Sport.* New York: Oxford University Press.

Lewis, Lisa. 1990. *Gender Politics and MTV: Voicing the Difference.* Philadelphia: Temple University Press.

Lipsitz, George. 1982. *Class and Culture in Cold War America: A Rainbow at Midnight.* South Hadley, Mass.: Bergin and Garvey.

———. 1988. *A Life in the Struggle: Ivory Perry and the Culture of Opposition.* Philadelphia: Temple University Press.

———. 1990. *Time Passages: Collective Memory and American Popular Culture.* Minneapolis: University of Minnesota Press.

Liscio, John. 1990. Say It Ain't So: Fraud Threatens the Baseball Card Boom. *Barron's,* March 19, 14.

Marc, David. 1984. *Demographic Vistas: Television in American Culture.* Philadelphia: University of Pennsylvania Press.

Marcus, George, and Michael M. J. Fischer. 1986. *Anthropology as Cultural Critique.* Chicago: University of Chicago Press.

May, Elaine Tyler. 1988. *Homeward Bound: American Families in the Cold War Era.* New York: Basic Books.

References

McRobbie, Angela. 1991. *Feminism and Youth Culture: From "Jackie" to "Just Seventeen."* Boston: Unwin Hyman.

Meiner, Dave. 1973. Hobby Publicity Improving. *Sports Collectors Digest,* October 26, 5.

———. 1974a. Sports Advocate. Note—Sports Publications Cool to Collectors. *Sports Collectors Digest,* May 15, 5.

———. 1974b. Sports Advocate. *Sports Collectors Digest,* May 31, 10.

———. 1974c. Sports Advocate. *Sports Collectors Digest,* July 7, 7.

———. 1974d. Sports Advocate. Inflation Rocks the Hobby. *Sports Collectors Digest,* July 15, 4–5.

———. 1974e. Sports Advocate. *Sports Collectors Digest,* November 15, 5.

———. 1975. Reflections of a Departing Hobby Writer. *Sports Collectors Digest,* May 31, 2–3.

Messner, Michael A. 1988. Sports and Male Domination: The Female Athlete as Contested Ideological Terrain. *Sociology of Sport Journal* 5 (3): 197–211.

———. 1990. Masculinities and Athletic Careers: Bonding and Status Differences. In *Sport, Men, and the Gender Order: Critical Feminist Perspectives,* edited by Messner and Donald Sabo, 97–108. Champaign, Ill.: Human Kinetics Press.

———. 1992. *Power at Play: Sports and the Problem of Masculinity.* Boston: Beacon Press.

Moores, Lew. 1973. Collecting Baseball Cards for Love and Money. *Cincinnati Post,* November 10.

Mortimer, Jeff. 1975. Fan in the Street. *Sports Collectors Digest,* October 31, 3.

Nardinelli, Clark, and Curtis Simon. 1990. Consumer Racial Discrimination in the Market for Memorabilia: The Case of Baseball. *Quarterly Journal of Economics* (August): 575–96.

Oriard, Michael. 1984. *The End of Autumn.* Garden City, N.Y.: Doubleday.

Pfeil, Fred. 1990. *Another Tale to Tell.* London: Verso.

Rader, Benjamin. 1984. *In Its Own Image: How Television Has Transformed Sports.* New York: Free Press.

Radway, Janice. 1984. *Reading the Romance: Women, Patriarchy, and Popular Literature.* Chapel Hill: University of North Carolina Press.

Reader Reaction. 1981a. *Sports Collectors Digest,* September 25, 6.

———. 1981b. *Sports Collectors Digest,* October 9.

———. 1981c. *Sports Collectors Digest,* October 23, 8.

———. 1981d. *Sports Collectors Digest,* November 6.

Rothenberg, Randall. 1989. Topps Makes a Move into Magazines. *New York Times,* December 22.

Sabo, Donald, Jr., and Ross Runfola. 1980. *Jock: Sports and Male Identity.* Englewood Cliffs, N.J.: Prentice Hall.

Salisbury, Luke. 1989. *The Answer Is Baseball: A Book of Questions That Illuminate the Great Game.* New York: Times Books.

Spigel, Lynn. 1990. Television in the Family Circle: The Popular Reception of a New Medium. In *The Logics of Television: Essays in Cultural Criticism,* edited by Patricia Mellencamp. Bloomington: Indiana University Press.

———. 1992. *Make Room for TV: Television and the Family Ideal in Postwar America.* Chicago: University of Chicago Press.

References

Stewart, Susan. 1984. *On Longing: Narratives of the Miniature, the Souvenir, the Collection.* Baltimore: Johns Hopkins University Press.

Stommen, John. 1973a. Our Hobby. *Sports Collectors Digest,* October 12, 3.

———. 1973b. Our Hobby. *Sports Collectors Digest,* December 28, 3.

———. 1976. Our Hobby. *Sports Collectors Digest,* October 15, 3.

Taylor, Jack. 1975. Baseball Cards: Big Money. *Detroit Free Press,* May 14.

Taylor, Ted. 1981. Court Gives Topps "Double Play" Decision. *Sports Collectors Digest,* September 20, 6–10.

———. 1990. Fleer: Double Bubble Busts the Trust. *Baseball Card Boom,* February, 26.

Teens Suspected of Stealing $15,000 in Baseball Cards. 1990. *Star Tribune* (Minneapolis), June 29.

Thefts in Sports Memorabilia on the Increase. 1990. *San Francisco Chronicle,* July 7.

Topps Company, Inc. 1987. *Prospectus,* May 21.

———. 1989. *Prospectus,* May 4.

Topps Corporation. 1972–86. Annual reports.

———. 1990. *Annual Report to the Securities and Exchange Commission for the Fiscal Year Ending March 3.* File number 0-15817, 4–9.

Topps: Baseball Bubble-Gum Maker to Launch Magazine Aimed at Card Collectors, Sports Fans. 1989. *Wall Street Journal,* November 17.

Topps Holder Group Plans Offering. 1988. *Wall Street Journal,* September 30.

Trotter, Joe William, Jr. 1991. *The Great Migration in Historical Perspective.* Bloomington: Indiana University Press.

Tudor, Caulton. 1975. Gum Cards Have Withstood Time, Tight Money. *Raleigh Times,* June 19.

Veblen, Thorstein. 1919. *The Theory of the Leisure Class: An Economic Study of Institutions.* New York: B. W. Huebsch.

Voigt, David Q. 1983. *American Baseball.* Vol. 3, *From Postwar Expansion to the Electronic Age.* University Park: Pennsylvania State University Press.

Weidman, Jerome. 1954. Weidman's Burden . . . Anybody Got a Solly Hemus? *Sports Illustrated,* August 16, 45.

Whitson, David. 1990. Sport in the Social Construction of Masculinity. In *Sport, Men, and the Gender Order: Critical Feminist Perspectives,* edited by Michael A. Messner and Donald Sabo, 19–29. Champaign, Ill.: Human Kinetics Press.

Will, George. 1990. *Men at Work: The Craft of Baseball.* New York: Macmillan.

Will Topps Offer a Piece of Gum with Every Share? 1989. *Wall Street Journal,* April 2.

Woodhull, Nancy. 1974. $1,500 for a Honus Wagner: Face Cards with High Prices. *Detroit Free Press,* June 22.

Index

Aaron, Henry (Hank), 29, 98
Allen and Ginter Tobacco Company, 3
Alomar, Roberto, 37
American Card Catalogue, The
   (Burdick), 129 n. 1
American Graffiti, 89, 91
American Sports Card Collectors
   Association, 78
Anderson, Torben, 128 ch. 2 n. 1
Angell, Roger, 5
Anson, Adrian, 37
antiwar movement, 87
Armurol Corporation, 18
Aronowitz, Stanley, 106–7
athletics. *See* sports
audiences. *See* sports spectatorship

baby-boom generation, 93, 110, 123
Bad News Bears, The, 91
Bailey, Mel, 80
Baltimore Orioles, 5, 109
Bang the Drum Slowly, 91
Barker, Charles, 80
baseball, 101–2, 104; and game
   attendance, 94, 130 n. 7; major-
   league, 17–18, 91–92, 94–95,
   118–19, 127–28 ch. 1 n. 2, 130 n.
   7; minor-league, 90, 94, 128 n. 3;

and national identity, 93–96; and
   nostalgia, 4–7, 26, 31, 76, 109–12;
   and race, 5–7, 36–37, 94–96. *See
   also* Major League Baseball Players
   Association (MLBPA); *and under
   specific teams and players*
Baseball Card Boom, 16, 17
baseball card collecting, 104; and
   bargaining, 31–32, 39; boundaries
   of, 45–46, 85; camaraderie in, 39;
   and community, 99; crime within,
   24–25; and divorce, 64–65; and
   gender identity, 47–49, 58–66,
   86–97, 110–15; history of adult
   hobby, 14, 16, 75–97, 129 n. 1; and
   money, 26, 45–46; and nostalgia,
   13, 14–15, 81–83, 85, 87, 128 n.
   4; and play, 107–8; and race, 7,
   127 intro. n. 2, 128 ch. 2 n. 1; role
   of newsletters in, 76; and romance
   reading, 71; trade conventions for,
   23, 78, 79. *See also* gender identity;
   race; sets, baseball card; sexual
   development, and collecting
baseball card collectors: class
   background of, 35–36; cynicism of,
   25; female, 58–59, 115–18; greed
   among, 42

Index

Index

Index

Robinson, Humberto, 82
Robinson, Jackie, 82, 94–95
romance reading, and collecting, 71
"rookie cards," 23, 47, 67
Rose, Pete, 67
Rosen, Alan "Mr. Mint," 24, 125
Ruth, Babe, 109

Salisbury, Luke, 98–99, 110–12, 114
San Francisco Giants, 5, 18, 119
Score (company), 18
Sedaka, Neil, 89
sets, baseball card, 13, 128 ch. 3 n. 2; collecting, 14, 47–74, 128 ch. 3 n. 1; "factory," 50; and gender differences, 64–66; and household space, 66; regional and promotional, 18
sexual development, and collecting, 58–63, 112, 113–14
Shoeless Joe (Kinsella), 5–6
Shorin, Abram, 19
Shorin, Ira, 19
Shorin, Joseph, 19
Shorin, Philip, 19
Simon and Garfunkel, 94
Simon, Curtis, 128 ch. 2 n. 1
Smith, J. J., 80
Solon, Bob, 80
Southwestern Ohio Sports Collectors, 78
Spahn, Warren, 29, 83
Spigel, Lynn, 53, 90, 104, 112
Spink, C. C. Johnson, 80
Sporting News, 77, 80
sports, 9–10, 15, 101; and gender socialization, 10–11, 58. *See also* gender identity; "male bonding"
Sports Americana Baseball Card Price Guide, The, 16, 17, 127 ch. 1 n. 1
Sports Collectors Digest (SCD), 83–85, 92–93, 129 n. 2; creation of, 76–79; and Dave Meiner, 83–85, 79; and industry development, 23, 24, 25–27, 78–79; sale to Krause Publications, 16–17, 26–27
Sports Illustrated, 52

sports spectatorship, 9–10, 49, 107–8; and gender identity, 10–13, 15, 35, 108–9, 119. *See also* baseball card collecting; gender identity; homosexuality, and collecting; "male bonding"; sexual development, and collecting
Star Wars, 20
Stewart, Susan, 12–13, 14
Stommen, John, 16–17, 26–27, 76–78
subcultures, 102, 104–6, 112–13. *See also* baseball card collecting
suburbanization, 7
Super Bowl, 9

television, 19–20, 90, 92. *See also* popular culture; *and under individual programs*
Texas Rangers, 5
Theory of the Leisure Class, The (Veblen), 11–12
tobacco companies, and baseball cards, 3
Topps baseball cards, 4, 21, 25, 36, 57, 90, 127 intro. n. 1, 128 ch. 3 n. 2; 1972 set of, 75, 78–79; representations of race on, 95
Topps Corporation, 69, 104; antitrust suit against, 17; and baseball card marketing, 4, 18, 19–22, 52, 57, 75, 81, 90, 128 ch. 3 n. 2; and representations of race, 95
Topps Magazine, 22
Trader Speaks, 77, 129 nn. 2–3

Untouchables, The, 91
Upper Deck baseball cards, 19
Upper Deck Company, 19, 22
urban life, 5–7, 36, 89–90

Valle, Frankie, 89
Veblen, Thorstein, 11–12
Veeck, Bill, 92
Vinton, Bobby, 89

Wagner, Honus, 80
Walker, Hershel, 30
Weidman, Jerome, 52–53
Will, George, 5, 49

Index

John Bloom is currently an assistant professor in the Department of American Studies at Dickinson College. His published work has examined sports as a popular culture phenomenon. He has drawn from the field of cultural studies to examine sports as a significant cultural location for the formation of subcultures, the exploration of cultural identities, and the negotiation of gender boundaries. Bloom's current work examines athletics at federally operated boarding schools for Native Americans.